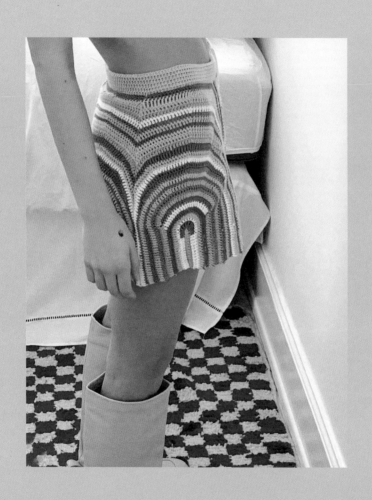

Hot Girl Crochet

Rose Svane

15 EASY
CROCHET
PROJECTS
FROM BAGS
TO BIKINIS

ilex

Contents

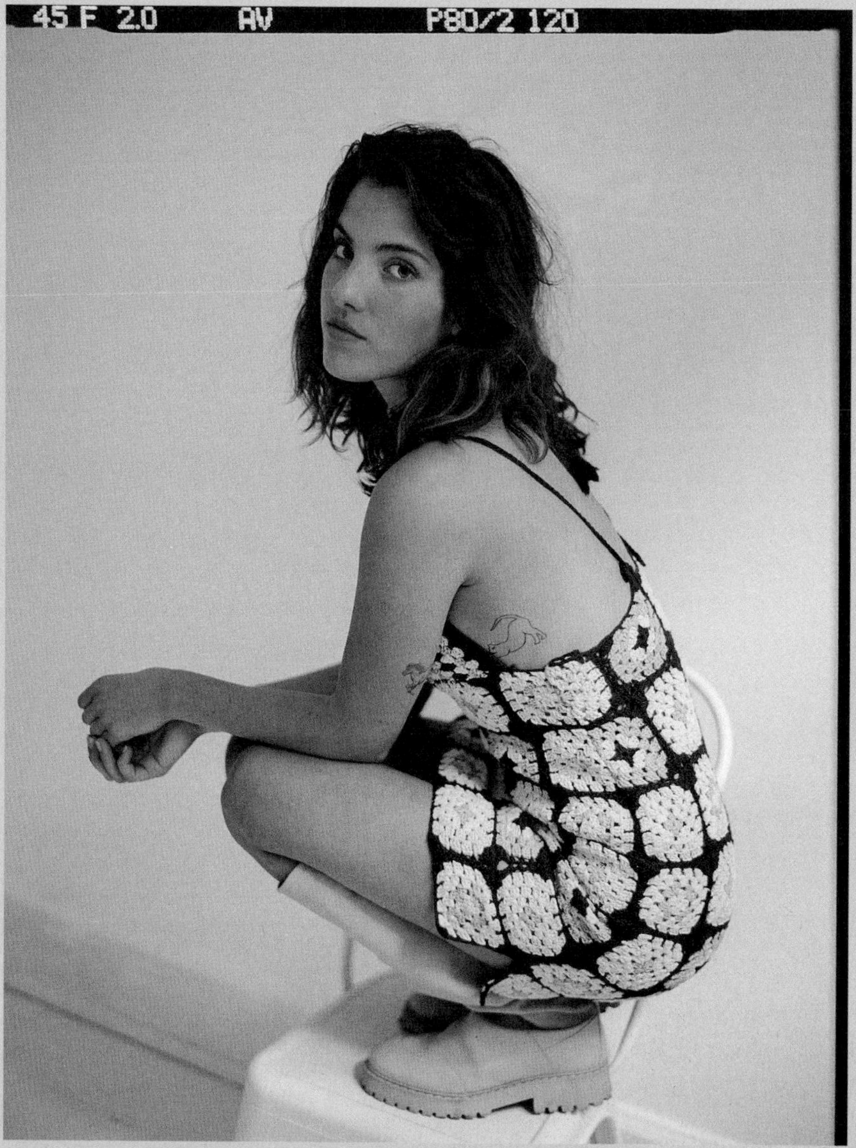
45 F 2.0
AV
P80/2 120

Foreword

Welcome to a world filled with all things crochet, loving support and eternal sunshine. This book takes you by the hand and guides you through lots of crochet techniques and a starter kit of patterns that I hope you will find inspiring. You'll find the tools you need to be able to reproduce the designs you see in the patterns section, but once you get more confident, there are infinite opportunities for you to get creative. Think of it like colouring in the pages of a colouring book – in this book, I am simply providing a collection of framework designs that you can then colour in any way you wish.

Think of my patterns as a kind of mental break from your hectic everyday life, a place of refuge where you can put your brain on standby and let your creativity flow – a kind of crochet mandala. This book is especially for those of you who are having a little trouble finding your place in this world and may be struggling with some doubt and uncertainty – just like the rest of us. Crochet creates a very special space, where you learn more and more about yourself with every stitch you make. However crazy this may sound, it was crochet that helped me to find myself and be at peace with who I am.

I could write several hundred pages about what crochet means to me and how it has helped me become the person I am today. However, I'll keep it short and only turn back the clock to my last three years at school. It was a particularly hard and unpleasant time for me. I found it extremely difficult to find my niche and I spent far too much time trying to fit my quirky personality into other people's boxes. I'm a people-pleaser, and I prefer to avoid conflict. As a confused teenager, I tried on a variety of different personalities, until I realized that none of them would ever suit me because they were all pretend and artificial. During those three tough years at school, my mother encouraged me to take up a creative hobby so that I could get a little distance from the enormous social pressure I was feeling and calm my racing thoughts. I'd never considered myself particularly creative and so I wasn't wild about the idea.

I've always struggled with not being good at things, and so I didn't even want to try anything new. However, after those three hard years of school followed by another couple of years when it felt like I was treading water, I finally picked up a crochet hook and some yarn because the universe told me that that's what I should do. My mother is a fascinating person and a skilful spiritual guide – she's a clairvoyant, healer and kinesiologist, she communicates with the dead and I sometimes suspect that she can also talk to animals – so when she makes a suggestion, I know deep inside that it's the best advice I'll ever get. She talks to the universe and acquires knowledge that helps me to get through life more easily. So, one day I cycled over to my grandmother's house with my hook and yarn. As my grandmother crochets, who else should teach me the craft but one of the most delightful women in my life?

I had a clear idea that the first thing I would crochet would be a lovely big blanket, like the one I had seen in a family photo from the 1970s. With a cup of coffee and great enthusiasm, my grandmother showed me how to make the first stitches. It looked easy, or so I thought. I quickly grabbed the hook and yarn myself and tried to copy what she was doing. But – ugh! – it was one of the most difficult things I'd attempted in ages. I wanted to cry. I have this annoying perfectionist sitting on my shoulder, laughing scornfully whenever there is something I just can't get the hang of, and that laughter doesn't stop until either I overcome the problem or I give up. So, I gave up. I put down the hook, drank the rest of my coffee and said, 'Thanks for your help, Granny, but I'll never be a crocheter.' As you have no doubt figured out, because you now have this book in front of you, this is not where the story ends. This book was written by a crocheter who definitely didn't give up. Instead, I gave it another go and crocheted day and night for a whole month, putting my social life on hold.

"After the article in *Cosmopolitan*, things really took off."

Before long, a girl from Spain contacted me via Instagram and asked where she could buy my crocheted items. I was puzzled; I didn't understand why on earth she wanted to buy some weird stuff that I had made. She stuck to her guns, and suddenly she wasn't the only one. A month later I received an email from someone who worked for *Cosmopolitan* magazine in the United States. They wanted to publish an article about one of my crocheted bags. I replied, 'Yes, please!' It was a frantic period and I remember that at the time I often cried happy tears, because it all seemed so unreal. I felt that I was being seen and recognized for what I loved doing most, for something I was doing to please no one other than myself.

After that article appeared in *Cosmopolitan*, things really took off. First, I was contacted by the brilliant photographer Renell Medrano. She wanted a very special skirt, inspired by a vintage Missoni knitted dress. This is probably still the hardest task I've ever been set, but it was great to have the chance to work with such an interesting person and create a beautiful, unique garment. While working on this skirt, I learned how to use certain crochet techniques that enable you to create little works of textile art, such as the granny square trousers on pages 266–267 and the skirt on pages 2–3. The day came when I finished the skirt and sent it off to Renell. No more than a few hours later, the American YouTuber

Emma Chamberlain – who I've always been a huge fan of, by the way – wrote and asked if she could buy one of my crocheted bags. It almost blew my mind.

Not long after, I could see that it was becoming popular for celebrities to wear handmade items from small brands or even homemade ones from individual makers, like me. This trend is still going strong and doesn't look like it will disappear any time soon. Homemade is the new black. So, grab some yarn and a crochet hook – maybe one day one of your idols will wear an item that you crocheted! But for me, the very best thing was finding out that thousands of people all over the world had found inspiration in what I'd been crocheting at home in my little room in Nørrebro, Copenhagen.

"Crochet is truly magical, and I hope everyone in the world tries it just once in their life."

I felt that my crocheted items and I were becoming part of something bigger, helping to create a fantastic, inspiring community. Crochet is the most meditative activity I have ever tried. It's cathartic and healing like therapy or a series of big, warm hugs. Just think of the power that crochet has! When I first became aware of the magic of the craft, it helped me make sense of things and I understood why crochet had to become a major part of my life – it was essential in enabling me to recover from a difficult period that had scarred my soul.

Crochet became, and it still is, a haven where I could please myself and where I am and have always been good enough, no matter what. In fact, I'm better than good enough. Nowadays I can laugh at the way I was back at my grandmother's house, when I almost threw the yarn and hook out of the window. But crochet isn't about being successful. It's about making loops and knots with a tool, however

banal that may sound, and creating something out of nothing with every stitch. Crochet is truly magical, and I hope everyone in the world tries it just once in their life.

If you are already a crocheter, you know how great it feels to wear an item of clothing or decorate your home with something you have made yourself. There is a little bit of self-love woven into every stitch, and you can really feel it. And if you haven't crocheted before, all I can say is, enjoy! You are about to learn the most wonderful craft, which can take you to a better place in life, and to a meditative and always inspirational universe. Be careful, though; you might never escape – or at least, not as the same person you were before.

Rose Svane
Copenhagen, 2022

Techniques

Choosing yarn

The yarn you choose to work with makes a significant difference to the look and feel of your finished crochet, so it's important to understand how different yarns behave. While the summary below is not an exhaustive guide to every type of fibre and yarn, it covers the basics and gives some useful tips. If you're new to crochet, read through this section first and you'll be well-prepared from the start.

Cotton

I'm a huge fan of cotton. Cotton fibres produce a smooth yarn that is not fuzzy, so you can very clearly see each stitch. However, cotton has little or no elastitcy and so it doesn't stretch or give very much, which means that it is a great choice for bags and pots, but it also means that it can be quite hard to work with. Cotton is extremely hard-wearing, which makes it a good choice for clothes, hats, cushions and blankets or rugs that will be used every day and need to stand up to wear and tear. Cotton comes in countless colours and qualities, including organic and recycled, and it's easy to source in yarn shops and online.

Cotton is a natural fibre, produced from the fluff that surrounds the seeds of the cotton plant. Cotton yarns come in many different weights, or thicknesses. I mostly work with the standard weights, which are 4-ply and double knitting (often abbreviated to DK). The different weights of yarn are referred to by different terms. Lace-weight yarns are generally the finest, but 4-ply and double knitting are both still relatively lightweight yarns. The ball band will always tell you the weight of the yarn. For the patterns where the instructions say you should use double knitting cotton yarn, it's fine work with two strands of 4-ply cotton yarn held together (although always work a tension swatch first). I often do that, as I find there's a much greater choice of pretty colours available in the lighter-weight yarns, which are often easier to find in the shops. To work with two strands, take one end from the centre of the ball and the other end from the outside of the ball. For patterns designed to be made in cotton yarn, see pages 102, 110, 128, 150, 160, 168, 180, 214, 224 and 248.

Raffia

Raffia is a fantastic yarn and I only wish I had discovered it sooner. Made from biodegradable wood fibres, raffia is a papery yarn that is water-repellent, which means it's great for making hats and beach bags that may get wet. Raffia is incredibly hard-wearing and will give your crochet a basketweave-like quality. I'll certainly be working with it much more in future.

Raffia comes in many different thicknesses. Finer, lighter weights are good for hats, while thicker raffia yarns are better suited for bags and baskets. You can also work with two strands of a finer-weight yarn (by holding two yarns together while crocheting) to make a thicker yarn. For a pattern designed to be made in raffia yarn, see page 192.

Wool

It was a while before I started crocheting with wool, but once I started, I quickly fell in love with it. Wool is very good for clothing, as it's a natural fibre that is warm and insulating. It is available in many different weights, and the qualities of each yarn depend on the breed of sheep, goat, alpaca, rabbit or other animal it comes from and how the yarn is manufactured. For patterns designed to be made in wool yarn, see pages 118 and 204.

Alpaca

Alpaca quickly became my favourite animal fibre yarn to work with because it's fine, soft and warm. It's made from the fleece of the alpaca, a relative of the llama native to Peru and Bolivia. Alpaca yarn is a bit like sheep's wool and, although it's finer in structure, it's just as strong as thicker sheep's wool. However, crocheted fabric made with alpaca yarn doesn't keep its shape quite as well and may stretch a bit over time, so when you're making a garment or anything else where the fit or size is important, bear this in mind when you're deciding which size to make. If you're deliberating between sizes, consider going down a size when working with alpaca. For a pattern designed to be made in alpaca yarn, see page 234.

T-shirt yarn

This is a fun, chunky yarn that looks a bit like string. It's known as T-shirt yarn because it's made using recycled jersey fabric that is often a byproduct of the fashion industry. If you're a beginner crocheter, I recommend you start by buying a ball of T-shirt yarn (preferably in a pale colour so it's easier for you to see your stitches) and then sit down and practice various stitches. This type of yarn is perfect for beginners because it's chunky and therefore requires a large crochet hook, which means you can quickly enjoy the results of your efforts.

T-shirt yarn is particularly well-suited for bulkier projects such as rugs, bags or the pouffe on page 138 of this book. It's also very durable, so if you want to make something that will withstand a lot of wear and tear, T-shirt yarn is a really good choice.

Crochet essentials

Crochet hooks

When you crochet, it's important to choose exactly the right crochet hook. I'm not just talking about the size of the hook here – we'll get to that on page 33 – but about the actual shape of its handle and grip (the sections of the hook that you hold while working). When I began crocheting, I bought a cheap set of 15 crochet hooks of various sizes for 20 kroner (a few pounds). There was nothing wrong with them and they would certainly work fine for some people, but I began to experience severe pain in my wrist and right elbow. If you spend many hours a day crocheting, it's worth experimenting with different styles of crochet hook. I have tried out many different types, from classic to ergonomic. The ones that suit me best are called Clover Soft Touch, which have a plastic handle and a rubberized thumb grip; since discovering this brand, I haven't used any other type. However, it's all about experimenting and making a note of what works best for you.

Stitch markers

Stitch markers look like plastic safety pins or paper clips and are used to mark a specific point in your crochet that you want to return to or pay particular attention to. For example, they may mark the place where you're going to increase the number of stitches when making sleeves. The markers act as a reminder, so you don't need to re-count stitches or keep track of more things than you can remember. I rarely used stitch markers when I learned to crochet and so I got used to doing without them; however, for some patterns, markers are essential in order to achieve the desired result.

You can buy stitch markers in every conceivable colour and design, from cupcakes and unicorns to skulls and ghosts, but you can also use things you already have lying around at home, such as hairpins, safety pins and paper clips. The most important thing is that whatever you choose to use as a stitch marker, it must be able to be opened and closed around a stitch. All too often, I've set off without markers and then, when I've been crocheting on the go, I've had to resort to using an earring as a makeshift marker instead. It works fine, I hasten to add. If you're an earring wearer like me, this means you always have a stitch marker on hand. Sometimes you need to be resourceful.

You do need to use a stitch marker when making Agnes's hat (pages 160–167), because the hat is worked in a spiral with no obvious start or end to each round. That means a stitch marker is necessary to indicate where each round starts. You insert the marker in the first stitch made and once you've worked the stitch before the one with the marker, you've completed a round. Remove the marker, work that stitch and then insert the marker in the stitch you've just made to mark the next round. Each round finishes just before the marker, and every new round starts when you move the marker to the new stitch.

Darning needles

Darning needles with a blunt end are a must. I recommend buying a good handful of them right now, because you're bound to end up losing a few. They're mainly used for weaving in the ends of yarn when finishing off a piece (see page 95), but they're also used for sewing together the pieces of a crochet project, which you can read about on pages 94–96. They come in various sizes, materials and colours but always have a blunt end that helps to avoid splitting the yarn when sewing up. When working with chunky yarn, I prefer using plastic needles for weaving in ends because plastic needles have bigger eyes, making them easier to thread. Metal needles are good for delicate projects worked in fine yarn, because they are easier to insert neatly into the work.

Tension

Before you embark on a new project, make sure you're using the right size of crochet hook to achieve the desired results. Each of my patterns gives you a guideline size of hook, which is the one that I used when making the sample you see in the photographs, but we all crochet differently – I crochet loosely, for example – so it's important to work a tension swatch in order to match the tension given in the instructions. I must admit that I was never the biggest fan of working swatches until I made an entire dress that ended up three sizes too big for me. I didn't bother to make a tension swatch or adjust the size of hook accordingly, I just jumped straight in, followed the pattern and soon found out just how important tension swatches are. For an absolute beginner, tension isn't the most important thing in the world – focus on teaching yourself how to work the various stitches first. But if you want to make clothes and achieve the correct size, it's essential to crochet a tension swatch to understand whether your personal tension is tight, loose or just right and whether you need to size up or down the crochet hook.

Crochet a tension swatch using the yarn weight and hook size given in the instructions and using the crochet stitch specified. The ideal number of stitches and rows to achieve is usually measured over a 10cm square, but it's best to make a swatch that is slightly bigger than 10 × 10cm as edge stitches can often be slightly tighter than the main body of the fabric. When you've made your swatch, count how many stitches you have horizontally over 10cm, then count how many rows you have vertically in 10cm. Each pattern states the number of stitches I had in my tension swatch and, depending on the number you have, it will indicate whether you should change to a larger or smaller hook size or simply use the size indicated.

Keep your tension swatches. You can attach a label saying which yarn and hook you used to make the swatch, as you may want to refer back to it. However, remember that as you become more proficient at crocheting, your tension is likely to change. You could always stitch the swatches together to make a patchwork.

Sizing

When you crochet clothes and accessories, such as hats, it's important that you work to the size that fits you – or your friend, or loved one, or whoever you crochet for. You can't always assume that because you usually wear a size medium, you should always make the size medium in the pattern. Achieving a good fit when you crochet depends on the combination of the yarn and the hook you're working with. Before you get started, it's crucial to crochet a tension swatch (see page 31) in order to be sure of the finished dimensions your work. In the patterns where you need to choose which size to make, there is guidance on how to measure your body. Often, it's really easy and many of the patterns can be adjusted as you work – there is also guidance about that. Crochet is very free and easy, so it's never too late to adjust various measurements as you go along.

When choosing the best size to make, all you need is a tape measure and a notebook to write down the measurements, so you always have them to hand. If you're between sizes, I recommend going down a size as most yarns will stretch with wear. For some patterns, you'll be working from clothes you already have in your wardrobe. In this case, of course, you won't need to measure yourself because your template is an item of clothing that you know fits you. It's a great way to crochet as – once you've got a little bit of experience – it gives you the chance to make exactly what you want and all you need is the template to work from. This may sound a bit confusing now, but the patterns that use this approach explain this method clearly, so you'll know what to do (see the patterns on pages 168 and 204).

If do you choose to freestyle with the design – for example, if you decide to make your own extremely long version of a skirt – then you won't be able to rely on the quantity of yarn given in the pattern. As a general rule, it's better to buy slightly too much yarn than too little as it's annoying to run out and then find that the shade you're using has sold out in the meantime. Many yarn shops are understanding about taking back any unused balls of yarn left over at the end of a project. Of course, you can always hold on to any leftover yarn in case the project ever needs adjusting or darning, or you can keep it for another exciting crochet project – that's what I do.

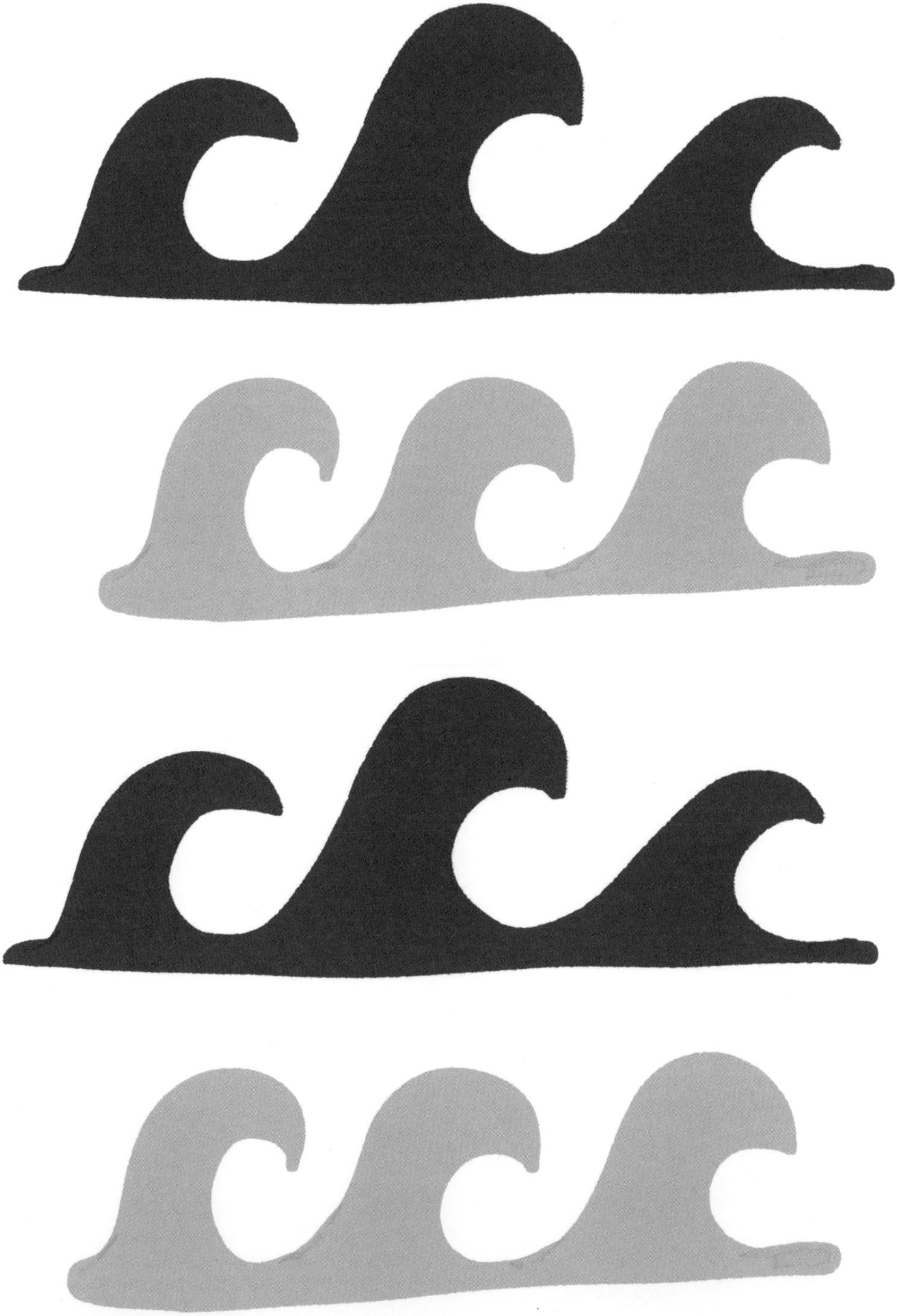

Holding the hook

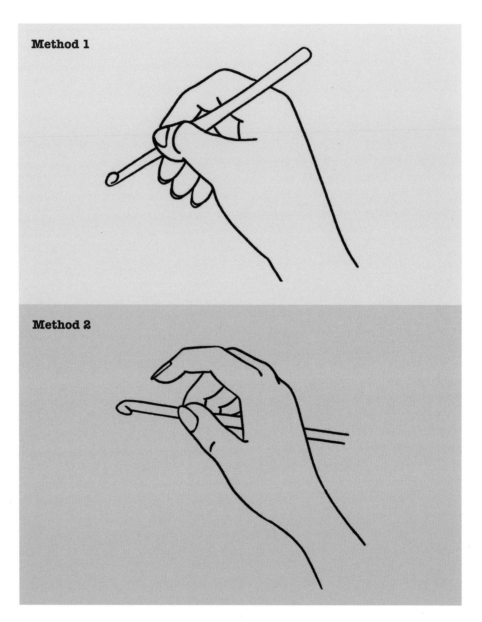

Method 1

Method 2

Crochet techniques

Holding the hook

There are two basic ways of holding the crochet hook. If you're a beginner, it's a good idea to try both methods and decide which one suits you best, as the most comfortable way of holding the hook varies from person to person.

Method 1:
Hold the hook in your right or left hand as you though you're holding a pencil, with your thumb and index finger on the grip and the handle resting in the crook of your hand.

Method 2:
Hold the hook in your right or left hand as though you're holding a knife when cutting food, with your thumb and index finger on the grip and with the handle pushing against the palm of your hand.

For both methods, it's important that the head or lip of the hook faces downwards when a stitch is being worked.

If you want to hold the hook in your left hand, your grip will be a mirror image of the illustration opposite. Not many people choose to crochet with their left hand, however, because almost all crochet patterns are written for working right-handed. Even if you're usually left-handed, it doesn't necessarily mean that you'll find it easier to crochet with your left hand when you're starting out as a beginner. Just experiment! Everything will feel completely wrong and difficult when you're a beginner anyway, no matter which hand you use.

Holding the yarn

Hold the working yarn with your left (or free) hand. Most crocheters wrap the working yarn around their little finger, then lace it through the other fingers before bringing it over the index finger. Again, experiment with different methods until you find the one that feels most natural to you. Your left hand controls the flow and tension of the yarn, which means that the more tightly you grip the yarn in your left hand, the firmer your crocheted fabric will be. You must apply some tension to the tail end of the yarn to be able to work the stitches. Depending on how you hold the working yarn, use either the second or third finger and thumb of your left hand to gently pull down on the tail end of the yarn. When you wrap the yarn over the crochet hook, pass the tip of the hook under the yarn so that the hooked end picks up the yarn from above and pulls it through the loop(s) of your work.

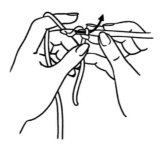

Starting a project

Most crochet projects begin with a slip knot or a magic ring. As well as starting a project, a slip knot is also useful when changing colours, as it ensures that the yarn doesn't get caught up in the colour change. A magic ring is the starting point for most crochet projects worked in the round. Maybe you want to make a hat or a round cushion where the crown or centre must be completely closed with no visible hole; this is when the magic ring is your friend.

Starting with a slip knot:

- With the yarn end on your right, unwind about 15cm of yarn. Make a loop of yarn, then insert the hook into the loop and pick up the yarn at the back of the loop in the lip of the hook.

- Pull the yarn through the loop and onto the shaft of the hook, then tighten the resulting knot. You now have one loop on the hook.

- Leave the tail end about 15 cm long, which can be used later for weaving in (see page 96).

Slip knot

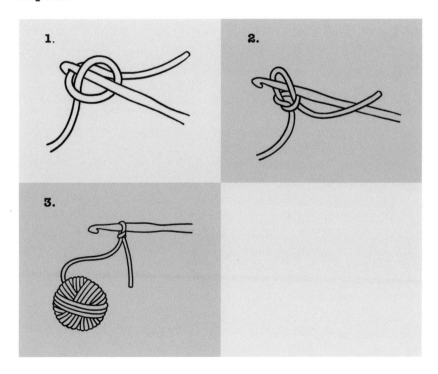

Starting with a magic ring:

- With the tail end of the yarn on your right, unwind about 15cm of yarn. Make a loop of yarn with the tail end of the yarn sat underneath the loop. Insert the hook into the loop and pick up the working yarn that is attached to the ball.

- Draw the working yarn caught in the throat of the hook through the loop so that there is now one loop on the hook, but do not pull the loop tight.

- Hold the initial loop of yarn (the magic ring) at the bottom between your thumb and second or third finger to keep it steady. Tension the working yarn with your index finger and then catch the working yarn in the hook to begin a chain stitch.

- Draw the working yarn through the first loop made on the hook to make a chain stitch and complete the magic ring. You now have one loop on the hook.

- Next, work the number of crochet stitches (here it's double crochet) given in the instructions into the ring. To do this, insert the hook through the magic ring and catch the working yarn in the hook.

- Draw the working yarn through the magic ring, so you now have two loops on the hook. Continue to complete the crochet stitch as usual. For double crochet, catch the working yarn in the hook without going through the centre of the magic ring, then draw it through both loops already on the hook to complete the stitch. You now have one loop on the hook.

- Follow the instructions to complete the number of crochet stitches needed so that they sit neatly along part of the magic ring.

- Take the loose tail end of the yarn and gently pull on it to close up the magic ring to leave the smallest opening possible.

Magic ring

1.

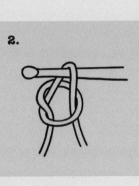

2.

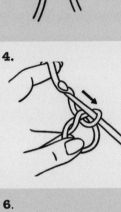

3.

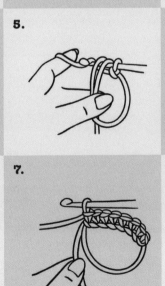

4.

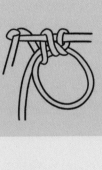

5.

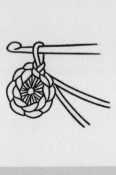

6.

7.

8.

Basic stitches

Here's an introduction to the most commonly used crochet stitches. Once you've mastered them, you will, in fact, be able to crochet almost anything. Crochet really isn't so hard after all...

Chain stitch

Chain stitch is mainly used to make the foundation row for any crochet project that is worked in rows. You start with a slip knot (see page 41) and then make a length of simple chain stitches. There will also be times when you will need to make chain stitches within a piece of crochet, such as turning chains at the end of a row that are necessary to keep the crochet at the correct height (see pages 57–59). Chain stitch is worked as follows:

- Make a slip knot so there is one loop on the hook. Catch the working yarn in the hook by encircling it anticlockwise (this is called yarn round hook or yarn over). Draw the yarn through the loop of the slip knot on the hook. If necessary, slightly rotate the hook to keep the yarn caught in the throat of the hook. This completes one chain stitch. Repeat this process – encircling the working yarn with the hook and drawing a new loop through the loop already on the hook – for each new stitch.

Starting a project with a row of chain

Projects often start with a foundation row of chain stitches. At the start of the instructions, the number of chain needed to begin will be specified. Count the chain stitch as you make each one, but it's always a good idea to doublecheck you've got the right number before continuing to crochet as these chain form the foundation for the project. When counting chain stitches, you never include the loop that remains on the hook and only count each V-shaped stitch below the hook. In the illustration of a row of chain opposite, three chain stitches have been completed and a fourth is in work.

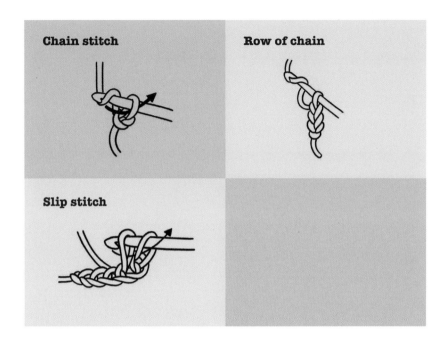

Chain stitch

Row of chain

Slip stitch

Slip stitch

A slip stitch is mostly used to join two stitches together neatly and invisibly; for example, at the end of a round of stitches when the last stitch needs to be secured to the first stitch and when stitches need to be decreased. Slip stitches can also be used to move from one point in the work to another, as they do not add height and are almost completely invisible. This can be useful, as you don't need to cut the working yarn and join on a new strand.

- Insert the hook into the stitch. Here, it's the second chain stitch from the hook. Pass the hook under only one strand of the chain.

- Encircle the yarn with the hook and draw it through both the strand of the chain stitch and the loop already on the hook. You now have one loop on the hook. This completes one slip stitch.Repeat this process for the number of stitches specified in the pattern.

Double crochet

A double crochet is a firm, dense stitch that can be worked in rows, rounds or a continuous spiral. It's very commonly used, as it's one of the easiest stitches to work, but it is not a particularly tall stitch, so completing an item in double crochet takes quite a bit longer than when using other, taller stitches. Double crochet is also a good way to finish off a project where you want a firm edge.

- Insert the hook into the second stitch from the hook. Pass the hook under only one strand of the chain. Encircle the working yarn with the hook and draw it through the first loop on the hook only, leaving the new loop and the original loop on the hook. You now have two loops on the hook.

- Encircle the working yarn with the hook once more and draw it through both the new loop and the original loop on the hook. You now have one loop on the hook. This completes one double crochet. Repeat this process for the number of stitches specified in the pattern.

- To work another row of double crochet, start with the working yarn at the right-hand edge. Make one chain stitch for the turning chain (see pages 57–59) – this doesn't count as a stitch but brings the work up to the same height as the double crochet stitches that are to follow. Work each double crochet stitch into both strands of the top of the double crochet stitches below.

Double crochet

1.

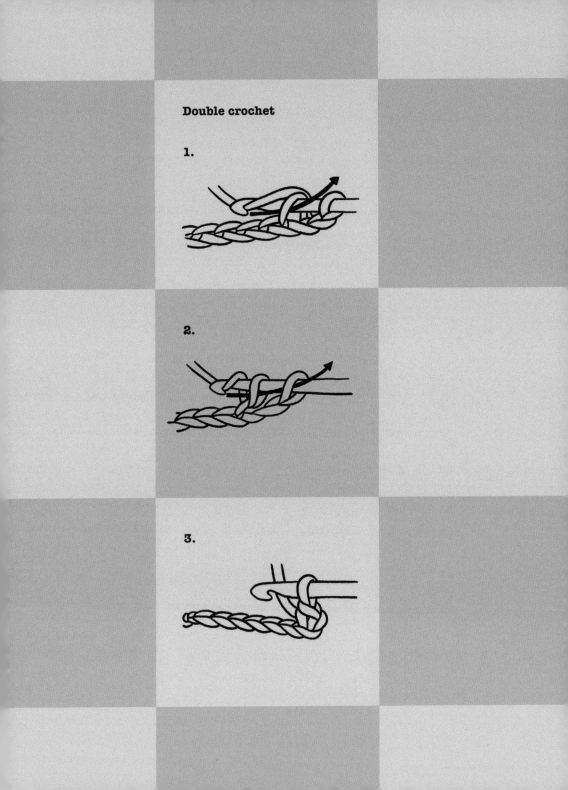

2.

3.

Half treble

1.

2.

3.

Half treble crochet

A half treble is a slightly taller stitch than double crochet, but it's only half as tall as treble crochet. It looks like double crochet and creates a similarly dense fabric, but half treble crochet is a little more fluid and so is good for many projects.

- Encircle the working yarn with the hook. Insert the hook into the third stitch from the hook. Encircle the working yarn with the hook again and draw it through the first loop on the hook only, leaving the new loop, the yarn round hook and the original loop on the hook. You now have three loops on the hook.

- Encircle the working yarn with the hook once more time and draw it through all three loops on the hook. You now have one loop on the hook. This completes one half treble crochet.

- Repeat this process for the number of stitches specified in the pattern, remembering to work yarn round hook before inserting the hook. To work another row of half treble crochet, start with the working yarn at the right-hand edge. Make two chain stitches for the turning chain (see pages 57–59) – this does count as the first half treble stitch of the row so you skip the first stitch at the base of the turning chain. Starting with the second stitch in the previous row, work each half treble crochet stitch into both strands of the top of the half treble crochet stitches below.

Treble crochet

1.

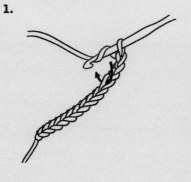

2.

3.

4.

Treble crochet

Treble crochet is the stitch you will encounter most frequently throughout the patterns in this book. It's a tall stitch, which means you see your work progress quickly. Trebles are used when making granny squares, for example, because these tall stitches can look like flower petals when worked in clusters (see pages 102–109).

- Encircle the working yarn with the hook. Insert the hook into the fourth stitch from the hook. Encircle the working yarn with the hook again and draw it through the first loop on the hook only, leaving the new loop, the yarn round hook and the original loop on the hook. You now have three loops on the hook.

- Encircle the working yarn with the hook again and draw it through the first two loops on the hook only, leaving the new loop and the original loop on the hook. You now have two loops on the hook.

- Encircle the working yarn with the hook once more time and draw it through the remaining two loops on the hook. You now have one loop on the hook. This completes one treble crochet.

- Repeat this process for the number of stitches specified in the pattern, remembering to work yarn round hook before inserting the hook. To work another row of treble crochet, start with the working yarn at the right-hand edge. Make three chain stitches for the turning chain (see pages 57–59) – this does count as the first treble stitch of the row and so you skip the first stitch at the base of the turning chain. Starting with the second stitch in the previous row, work each treble crochet stitch into both strands of the top of the treble crochet stitches below.

Double treble crochet

A double treble crochet is a double-height version of the classic treble crochet. Unlike treble crochet where you wrap the yarn round the hook once (see page 53), you start a double treble crochet by wrapping the yarn round the hook twice. Double treble crochet creates a very tall, open stitch that looks almost chain-like. It's a good stitch to use when working a lacy pattern.

- Encircle the working yarn with the hook twice. Insert the hook into the fifth stitch from the hook. Encircle the working yarn with the hook again and draw it through the first loop on the hook only, leaving the new loop, the two yarn round hook and the original loop on the hook. You now have four loops on the hook.

- Encircle the working yarn with the hook again and draw it through the first two loops on the hook only. You now have three loops on the hook.

- Encircle the working yarn with the hook again and draw it through the next two loops on the hook only.

- Encircle the working yarn with the hook one more time and draw it through the remaining two loops on the hook. You now have one loop on the hook. This completes one double treble crochet.

- Repeat this process for the number of stitches specified in the pattern, remembering to work yarn round hook twice before inserting the hook. To work another row of double treble crochet, start with the working yarn at the right-hand edge. Make four chain stitches for the turning chain (see pages 57–59) – this does count as the first double treble stitch of the row and so you skip the first stitch at the base of the turning chain. Starting with the second stitch in the previous row, work each double treble crochet stitch into both strands of the top of the double treble crochet stitches below.

'Infinite trebles'

For some projects, you may need to work stitches that are even taller than the double treble – a quadruple treble, for example. Luckily, once you know how to work a double treble (see page 54), you'll be able to make infinitely tall trebles. It's just a matter of how many times you wrap the yarn round the hook before inserting the hook into the stitch. So, if you want to make a quadruple treble, work as follows:

• Wrap the yarn round the hook four times. Insert the hook into the correct stitch.

• Wrap the yarn round the hook again and draw the yarn through the first loop only.

• *Wrap the yarn round the hook and draw it through two loops only.* Repeat this last step from * to * until there is one loop on the hook. This completes one quadruple treble crochet.

You'll come across plenty of asterisks in crochet patterns. They're used to avoid repeating instructions to save space. Wherever it says 'repeat from * to *', it means you must repeat the action(s) given in between the two asterisks.

Turning chains

A row of chain (see page 46) can be used to start a project, but chain stitches are also used to stand in for the first stitch at the beginning of a row. These stitches are called turning chains and they bring the hook up to the correct height for the stitches that are to follow. The number of turning chains varies according to the height of the stitch you're using for the project. The table below summarises how many turning chains are needed, depending on the stitch you're working. For example, if you're about to start a row of treble crochet (see page 53), you should first work three turning chain stitches, which will count as the first treble crochet stitch. The number of turning chains will typically be as follows:

Double crochet	1 turning chain
Half treble crochet	2 turning chains
Treble crochet	3 turning chains
Double treble crochet	4 turning chains

When you begin any project in rows, the instructions will tell you to make a specific number of chain (see page 46). You then work back and forth in horizontal rows and make a specified number of extra chain at the beginning of each row to act as turning chains. These instructions may sound confusing, but if you sit down and try making a swatch, they will make sense and you'll see the important role a turning chain plays. This is my top tip for all crocheters: sit yourself down and try to work through whatever it is that sounds confusing when written down. Everything always makes more sense when you have yarn and a crochet hook in your hands.

How to use turning chains

- To practice turning chains, we're going to work a swatch of treble crochet. Start by making 9 chain stitches (page 46) plus 3 extra chain. These 3 extra chain will act as the turning chain, as they will take the hook up to the same height as a treble crochet stitch, and count as the first treble. Next, work 1 treble crochet in the fourth chain from the hook. Remember, do not include the stitch on the hook when counting chain.

- There are now 2 treble crochet stitches that have been worked – although the first one is the 3 chain and the other one is the actual treble. Once you have completed the row by working 1 treble in each stitch of the chain, you'll have a total of 10 trebles – one actual treble for each of the 9 chain you cast on, plus the turning chain. You have now worked the first row and are about to work back along it.

- Turn the work so the working yarn is at the right-hand edge. Make 3 chain for the turning chain. These 3 chain count as the first treble of the second row. Work 1 treble in the next stitch of the previous row. Continue in treble crochet to the end of the row.

- Work the last treble of the second row in the third chain of the 3 chain in the previous row. The last treble of the row can be tricky, as the stitch of the previous row may be difficult to see.

It's a good idea to check the stitch count to make sure you have 10 trebles when each row is completed. To begin with, you may easily end up making too many or too few trebles. Keep practising!

Turning chains

1.

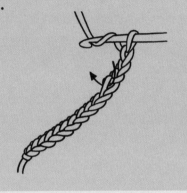

2.

3.

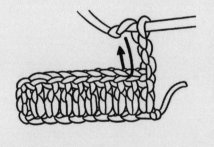

4.

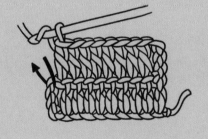

Working in rounds

If you aren't crocheting in rows, chances are you'll be working in rounds. Both flat circles and tube shapes are made in the round by crocheting into the top of the previous round without turning the work. Hats, skirts and some styles of bag are often worked in rounds. It's important to start and end each round in the correct place, otherwise the work can go badly out of shape. You might be instructed to start with a magic ring (see page 42), or you might need to make a foundation ring as outlined below. If you're using double crochet (see page 48), you work in rounds as follows:

- Make a length of chain (see page 46) with the number of stitches specified in the pattern instructions.

- Work a slip stitch (see page 47) into the first chain to form a foundation ring. This foundation ring may be very large, in which case you'll likely work upwards to form a cylindrical tube. Otherwise, the ring might be small and tightly closed, so you'll work outwards from the centre to make a flat, circular shape.

- To make a flat, circular disc, work 1 chain to stand in for the first double crochet. Next, work 1 double crochet either in the top of each of the chains of the foundation ring or into the centre of the ring itself, as shown in the illustration, following the instructions.

- Continue working double crochet either into the top of each chain or into the foundation ring until you're ready to complete the round.

- To complete the round, work a slip stitch in the top of the first double crochet worked at the beginning of the round. Continue in this way at the end of every round.

You can also start by making a magic ring (see page 42) and working the number of stitches specified into it. The same method applies: the first stitch is replaced by a specified number of chain and each round ends with a slip stitch in the top of the first stitch worked.

Working in rounds

1.

2.

3.

4.

5.

Stitch variations

Depending on what you've chosen to make, the basic stitches – chain, slip stitch, double crochet, half treble crochet, treble crochet and double treble crochet – may be worked in various ways to give the work a particular texture or look. These variations will also shape the work to give it the right dimensions. The almost infinite number of variations make crochet very free and easy, and a fun craft to learn. Here, I explain the four stitch variations that I use most frequently:

1. Working into the front or back loop

If you look at a stitch from above, you'll see that it is made up of two strands that together look like a V lying flat. The strand nearest to you is the front loop, while the strand furthest from you is the back loop. When crocheting, usually the hook is inserted through both the front and back loops. However, if you work into either the front loop or the back loop only, you have a stitch variation that can give your work shape. For example, this technique can be used to make the brim of a hat stand out a bit further in a particular direction from the rest of the hat. You can also use this technique to shape a basket by working into the back loop where the flat base of the basket turns into the upright sides.

Working into the front loop (in treble crochet)

Working into the back loop (in double crochet)

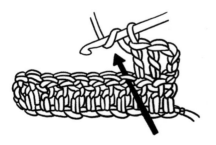

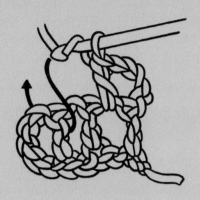

2. Working into the chain arch

In the instructions for items with a hole pattern, you will often be asked to work into the chain arch (see the patterns on pages 224 and 248). A chain arch is the name for a little row of chain that form a bridge between other stitches. When you are asked to work into the chain arch, it means that each time you come across such a row of chain (see page 46) into which you are to work, say, trebles (see page 53), you should work around the chain by inserting the hook under the whole chain instead into each individual stitch of the chain. This variation also often occurs in patterns made using granny squares (see pages 102 and 150). If you know a little bit about crochet, you will certainly have come across granny squares – which may be in the form of the classic square shape or granny-square stripes. The classic pattern, which looks almost like small flower petals, is created by working only into the chain arch and usually in groups of three trebles at a time.

3. Decreasing – working stitches together

Decreasing means reducing the number of stitches in the row or round. The simplest way to decrease is by working stitches together. The method of decreasing differs, depending on the crochet stitch you're working, but here are the three methods for the most common stitch types:

Method 1: Decreasing in double crochet

• Work to the point of the decrease. Insert the hook into the first stitch, wrap the yarn round the hook and draw it through. You now have 2 loops on the hook.

• Insert the hook into the next stitch, wrap the yarn round the hook and draw it through. You now have 3 loops on the hook. Wrap the yarn round the hook again and draw it through all 3 loops.

• You have worked a decrease by working 2 double crochet together to make 1 double crochet.

Method 2: Decreasing in half treble crochet

• Work to the point of the decrease. Wrap the yarn round the hook, then insert the hook into the first stitch, wrap the yarn round the hook and draw it through. You now have 3 loops on the hook.

• Insert the hook into the next stitch, wrap the yarn round the hook and draw it through. You now have 4 loops on the hook. Wrap the yarn round the hook again and draw it through all 4 loops.

• You have worked a decrease by working 2 half trebles together to make 1 half treble.

Method 1: Decreasing in double crochet

1.

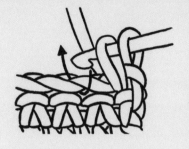

2.

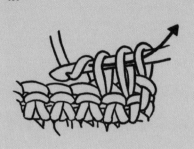

Method 2: Decreasing in half treble crochet

1.

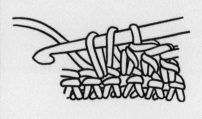

2.

Method 3: Decreasing in treble crochet

1.

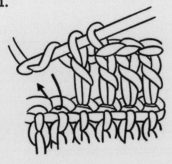

2.

3.

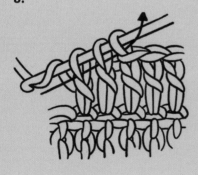

Method 3: Decreasing in treble crochet

- Work to the point of the decrease. Wrap the yarn round the hook, then insert the hook into the first stitch, wrap the yarn round the hook and draw it through. You now have 3 loops on the hook. Wrap the yarn round the hook and draw it through the first two 2 loops. You now have 2 loops on the hook.

- Wrap the yarn round the hook and insert the hook into the next stitch, wrap the yarn round the hook and draw it through. You now have 4 loops on the hook. Wrap the yarn round the hook again and draw it through the first two 2 loops. You now have 3 loops on the hook.

- Wrap the yarn round the hook again and draw it through all 3 loops.

- You have worked a decrease by working 2 trebles together to make 1 treble.

4. Increasing – working multiple stitches into the same stitch or space

Increasing is much easier than decreasing, no matter which crochet stitch you are working. The simplest way of increasing is by working two or more stitches into the same stitch or space in the row below, thus increasing the number of stitches in the current row or round and making the work larger. It's as easy as that. Quite often, increases are paired – in other words, the same increase is made at both the beginning and end of a row, so that the work grows evenly.

Tip!

This is my key tip for all crocheters:
every pattern instruction makes more sense
when you've got yarn and a crochet hook in
your hands. So, sit yourself down and take
the time to make a swatch and work through
whatever written instruction is confusing you
– hopefully, it'll make much more sense when
you can see what each instruction means.

If you're ever completely lost, go on YouTube.
It's a great resource for tutorials on how to
work the various stitches and techniques.
Because I didn't always have my grandmother
beside me to ask, watching YouTube tutorials
was how I learned some of those tricky
crochet techniques.

Reading charts

If you're a visual learner, like me, a colour chart or a stitch diagram can make crochet instructions easier to understand as it gives an immediate visual representation of what the finished piece should look like. Sometimes these charts and diagrams are used alongside more conventional written instructions, but increasingly patterns are being conveyed in these visual means, as they can be universally understood, so you can crochet in any language.

Presented in the form of a grid, charts are mostly used for complex colourwork and filet crochet when the design is best represented as an image. With a colour chart, each square represents a stitch or group of stitches, and the chart explains what colours are used for each of these and how they relate to each other to make up a colour motif or repeat pattern. When working filet crochet, a chart will explain where a square should be worked as an open mesh and where it should be worked as a solid block, again to make up a motif or repeat pattern.

Stitch diagrams are made up of a series of symbols, with each crochet stitch being represented by a symbol. These symbols approximate the shape and size of the actual stitch. Each stitch diagram is accompanied by a key to these symbols. The stitch diagram tells you when to work each stitch, with every row and round numbered so that you know which direction to work in. When working in rows, you start at the bottom left-hand corner with the foundation chain. Follow the row numbers from the bottom of the diagram to the top. Usually, odd-numbered rows run from right to left and even-numbered rows run from left to right. Each row may be linked with a turning chain. When working in rounds, you usually work outwards from the centre.

When working from a stitch diagram, you must work a stitch for every symbol shown. Some stitch diagrams have a bottom line with a star next to it. This line with a star indicates a row that you've already worked: you don't need to work it again, it's just there to indicate the stitches you'll be working into.

Each chart or diagram in this book has been given a name, for example, A.1 or A.2. When a pattern features more than one chart or diagram, the instructions will tell you which one to use when.

Reading a stitch diagram when working in rounds

When you're working in rounds and following a chart to make a flat circular piece, you should read the chart outwards from the centre, following the ascending round numbers. The rounds will appear as concentric circles, starting small in the centre and getting wider as they grow outwards, just like the crochet piece.

If you're working a tube of crochet in a repeat pattern, you'll have to repeat often a stitch diagram. This means that once you've worked one round of the diagram from right to left, you need to start again from the beginning and work another round from right to left, following the same instructions. The number of times you need to repeat any round will be indicated in the instructions.

Reading a stitch diagram when working in rows

When working in rows, read the chart from the bottom up. The key thing about working in rows is that, after completing each row, you change the direction in which you read the diagram. Right-side rows (when the right, or outward-facing, side of the work is facing you) are read from right to left. Wrong-side rows are read from left to right. There may not be a clear right and wrong side, so the first line of the chart will always be the one that determines which is the right side of the piece you're making.

When the instructions for a single row involve following more than one chart across that row, the order in which the charts are worked will also change depending on whether the right side or the wrong side is facing. For example, on a row that uses two charts, you should work chart A.1 first followed by A.2 on a right side row, then A.2 first followed by A.1 on a wrong side row in order to maintain the correct repeat pattern. As before, you don't count the line with the star next to it when counting the number of right-side and wrong-side rows. The first line above the starred row will be the right side and the following row will be the wrong side, and so on.

Reading colour charts

Colour charts are simple diagrams that convey which colours
should be used to create a motif or repeat pattern in your work.
As with the other charts, the starred line has already been worked
and you should start with the row above it. Every square of a colour
chart counts as one stitch, and every time a new colour appears you
should change the colour of your yarn. Before starting on a pattern
containing a colour chart, you need to know how to change to a
different-coloured yarn. You can read about this on pages 87–90.
Below is an example of a colour chart.

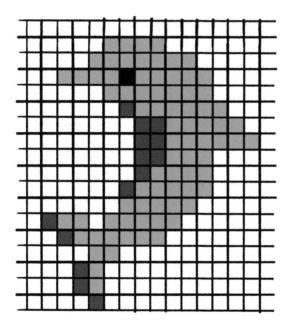

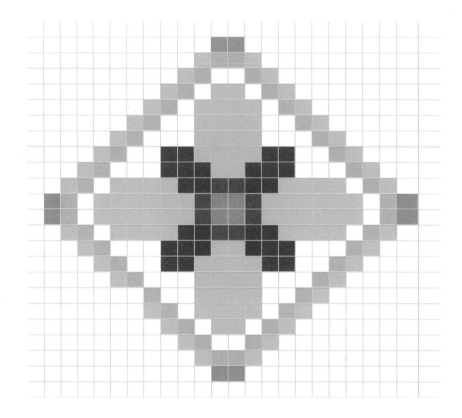

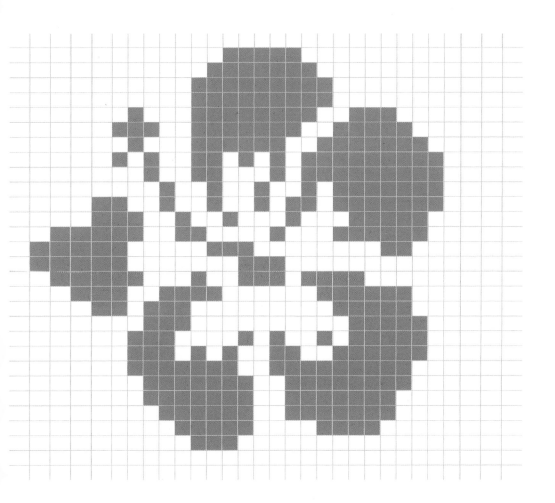

Choosing and changing colours

Choosing colours was never my strong point, so I often asked other people for advice on combining colours. If you're in doubt about which colours to choose, my best advice is to phone a friend – or text them if, like me, you're not the world's biggest fan of talking on the phone. There have been times when nothing has worked for me, and that's when I contacted a handful of my favourite people, because it's interesting to hear which colours others would choose for a particular project. However, I've recently discovered two methods that work well for me and help me to create lovely colour combinations.

My first method is actually a meditation exercise. I think everyone should try it, as meditation is always a good idea. This exercise is simple and yet not exactly easy. It's entirely a matter of using your intuition. Put on some music, perhaps your favourite song, some calm meditation music or something quite different – it can be anything, as long as it inspires you. There is one particular song that really unlocks the creative part of my brain: 'California Dreamin'' by José Feliciano is always a winner for me, but I also like to investigate different types of music and make a note of how it affects me. Close your eyes, breathe deeply and try to clear your mind of all thoughts. If that's difficult, try observing any thoughts that occur and let them pass by. Imagine that you are being handed some paints. They may be served up in tubes or pots or they might flow freely behind your closed eyelids. Maybe you can see lots of colours or perhaps only one. Welcome them all and remember every one of them, so that you can make a note when you're ready to open your eyes again.

It's possible that you'll sit there with your eyes closed and not see any colours. That's how it was for me to begin with, when my grandmother taught me this method many years ago. Later, my mother helped me to work on my intuition every day, and now the colours flow to me easily whenever I close my eyes. It took me a while to learn this and I can't be sure that this method will work for everyone, but I really like the idea of allowing my intuition to guide me in the choice of colours.

My second method is a little more concrete. Put on a good film and have a pencil and paper to hand. If you focus on the colours on the screen, you'll soon realize how many beautiful colour combinations appear in the film, either in the scenery, a room set or perhaps in the costumes of the characters. Countless times I've forgotten to follow the plot of a film because there was so much good colour inspiration to absorb from the scenes.

I'm lucky enough to live next door to my uncle, who is the biggest film nerd I know. We have a film club once a week to watch a film we think we should both see before we die. These film evenings have long been my haven of peace, where I sit down not with some

Tip!

Whenever you see a colour combination you love in a film, make a note. It's also a good idea to jot down the time at which the scene appears in the film, so you can always go back and be inspired by it all over again.

crochet or my phone in my hands, but with a load of peanut butter ice cream, and I allow myself to be absorbed in the world of cinema. You'll see references to films in the names of some of my patterns, because these designs were inspired by a particular film. On page 258 there is a list of the films that have given me inspiration for my crochet.

Maybe neither of my methods will work for you, or maybe you don't need a method, because you have always been good at combining colours. Whatever helps you to choose colours or be inspired in general, it's all about finding out what works for you. If you haven't used the Pinterest app yet, I recommend you download it right now. It's filled with inspiring images that you can always have at hand, and the platform is friendly and an easy way to find inspiration for your projects.

Changing colours

My designs are really colourful, so depending on what project you're making, there are likely to be plenty of colour changes. But even if there are no colour changes and the project is made all in one shade, you'll still need to know how to add in a new ball of yarn and move from working with one strand to another. Here are three methods for adding in a new yarn:

Method 1: Adding in a new yarn at the end of a row (illustrated on page 88)

This method creates the most invisible change from one colour of yarn to another. I have used this method a lot, because the change remains firm and won't unravel. You can change colour at the end of a row or in the middle of the work.

This technique creates the most invisible change from one strand of yarn to another in the last stitch at the end of a row. I use this method a lot, because the join remains secure and the work doesn't unravel.

- Work to the last stitch of the row where you need to change yarn. Start working the last stitch in the usual way with the existing yarn, but don't make the last yarn round hook so the stitch is partially worked but not completed.

- Make a slip knot (see page 41) in the new yarn and slide it onto the hook. Draw the loop of the new yarn on the hook through the stitch to complete it.

- Break off the old yarn (unless you're going to reuse it later on in the work), leaving an end of 10–15 cm.

- Now, continue to work with the new yarn. It's good practice to work over the tail ends of both yarns to fasten them into the back of the work, which means you don't have to do it all at the end.

**Method 1
Adding in a new yarn
at the end of a row**

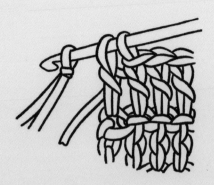

**Method 2
Adding in a new yarn
at the start of a round**

**Adding in a new yarn
at the start of a row**

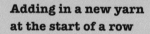

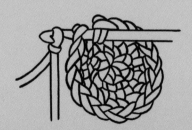

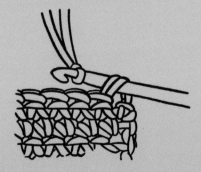

Method 2: Adding in a new yarn at the start of a round or row (illustrated opposite)

This is a good method to use when you've completed a round or a row and need to change yarn before starting the next round or row.

- Work to the first stitch of the round or row where you need to change yarn. Insert the hook into the first stitch of the new round or row.

- Make a slip knot (see page 41) in the new yarn and slide it onto the hook. Draw the loop of the new yarn through the place where you inserted the hook.

- If necessary, work the number of chain (see page 46) needed to start the new row or round. You're now ready to continue working with the new colour.

- Break off the old yarn (unless you're going to re-use it later on in the work), leaving an end of 10–15 cm. With this method, the tail ends of both yarns are left hanging from the work. The pattern will give instructions for fastening off these ends (see the patterns on pages 102, 110, 138 and 214).

Method 3: Adding in a new yarn with a knot

If you don't mind your finished crocheted piece looking a little random, this method is so simple. It's the easiest technique, as it involves nothing more than tying the old and the new yarns together with a knot. Any colour change will just happen by itself when you continue working past the knot, transitioning from the old yarn to the new yarn. You can choose to make a feature of any visible colour change by leaving the knotted yarn ends hanging from the right side of the work (see page 204) or you can crochet over the ends on the wrong side so that they are neatly concealed within the work.

Changing two or more colours and concealing the ends in the work:

You can change colour or yarn regardless of whether you're in the middle or at the beginning or end of a row or round. This method changes yarns and at the same time conceals the yarn ends in the work as you go. You should follow this method for the projects in this book that are worked in colour patterns (see pages 118, 128, 160 and 180).

- Work to one stitch before where you need to change yarn, but don't make the last yarn round hook so the stitch in progress remains incomplete.

- Make a slip knot (see page 41) in the new yarn and slide it onto the hook. Yarn round hook and draw the loop of the new yarn through the stitch to complete it. You're now ready to continue working with the new yarn. Break off the old yarn (unless you're going to re-use it later on in the work), leaving an end of 10–15 cm.

- Holding the yarn ends closely along the previous rows, work over both yarn ends (the new yarn and the old yarn) with the new stitches in the new yarn. This way, you work over the yarns you're not using and the ends are concealed at the back of the work. Once finished, trim the yarn ends that have been worked over to neaten, but not too close to the stitches as they may eventually unravel.

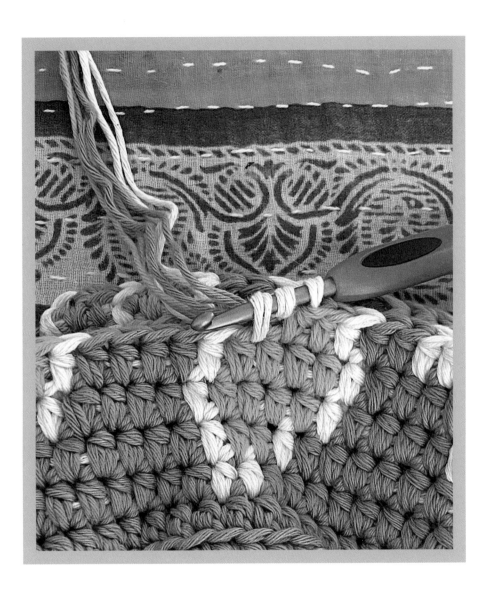

Finishing projects

At some point, all crochet projects have to be finished off, even though this can be one of the most boring things in the whole world to do. I have at least 20 unfinished crochet items lying around in baskets, boxes and bags because I can't bring myself to finish them, and they'll probably stay there for a good while longer. I've always felt that it's much more fun to begin a new project than finish off one that I've started to tire of, but there's also nothing as satisfying as seeing the finished fruits of your labours.

I've already shown how yarn ends can be concealed into the back of a project as you work. Because of this technique, the Never-Ending Blanket, which you'll find on page 102 of this book, is a wonder project because it doesn't need to be finished. It'll never be hidden away giving me a guilty conscience.

However, for those projects that do need finishing, here are the most important things you need to know when you get to that point:

**Method 1:
Joining seams with double crochet**

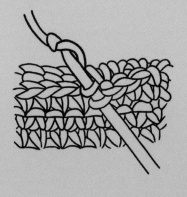

**Method 2:
Joining seams with backstitch**

Fastening off

Once you've finished crocheting any piece, you need to fasten off the stitches securely so that the whole thing doesn't unravel. When you have completed the last round or row, there'll be one loop left on the hook. Break off the yarn, leaving about 30cm, then wrap this yarn round the hook and draw through the last loop on the hook. Slide the hook out of the new loop and pass the yarn end through, then pull on the yarn end to make a tight knot that secures the stitches.

Assembling your work

When it comes to assembling your work – that is, joining pieces of crochet together – there are various ways of going about it. I'll guide you through the two methods I like best: joining seams with either double crochet or backstitch. It's a good idea to use the same yarn you used to crochet the project, as this will make seams less visible.

Method 1: Joining seams with double crochet (illustrated opposite)

This is my preferred seaming method, which I use as often as I can. It's easy and quick to do – which is really welcome when you're in that final phase of your project – and the resulting seam looks nice. When seaming with double crochet, I recommend using the same size hook you used for the project. Others think it's sensible to go down half a hook size, so just try it out for yourself. To join two pieces using double crochet, work as follows:

• Place the crochet pieces to be joined right sides together; this way the double crochet stitches used to assemble the project won't show on the right side. However, if you want a visible, external seam that makes a feature of the double crochet stitches, place the crochet pieces to be joined wrong side together. (The instructions should explain how to tell the difference between the right and wrong sides.)

- Make a slip knot (see page 41) in the yarn to be used for seaming, then slip it onto the hook. Insert the hook through both front and back loops of both pieces to be joined and work a double crochet (see page 48). Continue seaming in this way, moving forward by one stitch and working over the edges of the pieces you want to join together.

- When you have finished the seam, break off the yarn and weave in the yarn ends at both the beginning and end of the seam (see page 96).

Method 2: Joining seams with backstitch (illustrated on page 92)

Joining seams with backstitch can be time-consuming, but you're rewarded with a less visible seam in return. Because backstitch results in a firm, sturdy seam, it's good for sewing together bags, cushions and other projects where seams need to be strong, such as the shoulder seams of garments. To join two pieces using backstitch, work as follows:

- Thread a blunt-tipped yarn needle. Place the crochet pieces to be joined with right sides together. (The instructions should explain how to tell the difference between the right and wrong sides.)

- Secure the yarn at the right-hand edge by making a few small oversew stitches in the same spot (the first stitch in the row) and pass the needle through to the back of the pieces (furthest way from you). Next, bring the needle up through both pieces to the front of the work (closest to you), taking the yarn forward by two crochet stitches. Pull the needle to bring the yarn through, but not making the yarn too taut.

• Take the yarn backwards by one crochet stitch, passing the needle through to the back. Pull the needle again to bring the yarn through.

• Bring the needle up again, moving the yarn forward by two crochet stitches. Then take the yarn backwards by one crochet stitch, passing the need through to the back. Pull the needle again to tighten up the yarn. Continue seaming in this way, moving forward by two stitches, then going backwards by one stitch.

There are other ways to join crochet pieces, including mattress stitch and whip stitch; of course, you should choose the method that works best for you or is best for the project. You can also do as I did when I started crocheting and sew backwards and forwards anywhere you think there are a few stitches missing. There's often no right or wrong way to assemble a project. The most important thing is that the seams are strong and won't give way, so your crochet items will last.

Weaving in ends

Even though you've worked the last stitch of your project, you won't have completely finished until all the yarn ends have been woven in. I do it in the way that works for me and none of my projects have ever come apart. To weave in yarn ends, work as follows:

- Thread a blunt-tipped yarn needle with the yarn end to be woven in.

- Pass the needle through the back loops of a number of stitches, making sure that the yarn isn't visible from the right side. Weave the yarn through as many stitches as you think necessary for the work not to unravel and the ends be helf firmly in place; as a general rule, I weave through around 10 stitches.

- Trim the yarn ends to neaten.

Once you've woven in the yarn end of the last crochet stitch, you must also weave in the yarn ends where you've changed colour or joined in a new yarn. You can do this with a blunt-tipped yarn needle, as described above. Alternatively, you can conceal these ends as you work by crocheting 5–10 stitches over the loose ends (see page 87), then trimming the yarn ends to neaten.

Washing and care

If you use and wear your crochet creations as much as I do, you will probably want to wash them occasionally. It is important to look after them carefully and wash them exactly as recommended by the yarn manufacturer. It is a good idea to keep a ball band from the yarn you used for each project, so you know how to wash the finished article. This will tell you how the yarn should be washed, so that it won't shrink, lose its shape or disintegrate.

I wash quite a lot of my cotton crochet projects (see page 25 for more on cotton) in the washing machine, using the cold handwash programme (15–20°C), and that works fine – the clothes get clean without shrinking, losing their shape or falling apart. It is also a good idea to wet block or steam block crochet made of cotton. This will give a nice, smooth finish. To wet block a crocheted item, you start by soaking it in lukewarm water. Remove the excess water by placing the item between two towels and gently rolling it up, then lay your work out flat on a towel and stretch or smooth it to exactly the right shape before letting it dry. Steam blocking means that you lay the work out on a towel as above, but you use a steam iron or garment steamer to enable the steam to permeate the fibres. You should never press your crochet by placing an iron directly on it, as some types of yarn cannot tolerate heat and may disintegrate. That's a risk I dare not take. Wet or steam blocking are the safe options.

I wouldn't recommend washing, steaming or pressing crocheted articles made from wool or some other natural fibres (see page 24 for more about various natural fibres). Wool basically cleans itself; it doesn't really need to be washed – all it needs is to be hung up to air if necessary. If you do need to remove a stubborn stain, you can do so very carefully by laing the article out flat on a towel, dabbing the mark with a little stain remover and leaving it for a couple of hours or even overnight. Then rinse the part of the crocheted fabric with the stain remover on it in cold water and lay the article out flat again to dry, making sure that the wet area doesn't curl up, so that the work doesn't lose its shape.

Patterns

Home

I have always wanted my home to be the kind of place where people feel welcome and comfortable. It's also hugely important to me that a new person should be able to come into my home and immediately understand what kind of person I am, just by looking at my décor and furnishings. I'm not sure why this means so much to me, but I would hate for my home to appear to be something it's not. It has to be as genuine as possible.

For many years, more years than I have been crocheting, I longed for lovely crochet blankets and cushions, but never found any that were just 'me'. When I had been crocheting for some time, I realized that I could create things myself that would make my home reflect even more of my personality.

Crocheted home furnishings add warmth and atmosphere to an interior, and they create such a strong sense of personality because these items were made by you, in your favourite colours and with your energy.

The never-ending blanket

Crochet blankets have to be some of the most beautiful things
I have ever seen. Designing and making one myself has always been
a dream of mine. Ever since I started crocheting, I have kept my
notebook and pencil at hand whenever I watched a film inspired
by or dating from the 1970s, ready to make sketches of the many
lovely blankets and rugs that popped up in those films. I have many
dream projects involving crochet blankets, but this one – the Never-
Ending Blanket – is a good place to start. It's a great pattern for
beginners. It's simple, easy to follow and good practice for learning
how to read the instructions for other patterns, because making
this blanket will help you to understand many of the basic crochet
techniques. I call this type of crochet project a never-ending project,
because you will basically never come to the end of it. You can put
it down anytime and then pick it up again and carry on working on
it. It won't be finished at any particular point. You can go on forever,
if you want to, and while you're working on this blanket, it can lie
there looking lovely, adding warmth and atmosphere to the room.

Materials
- 100% cotton in DK weight
- Infinite quantities of yarn in an infinite number of colours
- 4.5 mm crochet hook

Tension
10 × 10 cm = 15 treble crochet in width and 8 rows in height.

If you have more stitches and rows to 10 × 10 cm,
change to a larger hook.

If you have fewer stitches and rows to 10 × 10 cm,
change to a smaller hook.

Worth knowing before you start
This blanket is worked in rounds from the centre outwards
in groups of trebles to make a classic granny-square pattern.
Traditional granny-square instructions usually tell you to work
chain stitches after each group of trebles. I have chosen to omit
the chain stitches (except at the corners), which gives the blanket
a denser structure. I also chose to use a relatively small hook
(4.5 mm), as I wanted a thick, heavy blanket. Of course you can
always go up to a larger hook size if you want a blanket that looks
thinner and lighter.

Techniques
Each treble at the beginning of a round is replaced by 3 chain.

Every round finishes with a slip stitch in the third chain you
worked at the beginning of the round.

You can make the blanket in a single colour or with as many colour changes as you fancy. If you decide to change colour, you should join your new colour after a completed round. When I join a new colour, I tie the two ends in a knot and work over them for the first 3 to 6 stitches of the new round. When you've worked over them you can cut off the ends. That way, you weave in the ends as you go along and you won't have to do it at the end.

You can also decide to join the new colour with a slip knot and crochet over the end from the previous round. If you're not sure what to do, turn to pages 87–90 and read up about changing colours.

Instructions

The never-ending blanket

1. Make 4 chain and work 1 slip stitch in the first stitch to make a ring. If you aren't sure about how to do this, turn to page 62 and read up on working in rounds.

2. Work 3 chain (counts as 1 treble), work 2 trebles into the ring you have just made and made 1 chain, *work 3 trebles in the ring you have just made and make 1 chain.* Repeat from * to * 2 more times. When you're about to finish the round, remember to join the first and last stitches with a slip stitch in the third chain you worked at the start. When the round is complete you have 4 groups of 3 trebles.

3. On the next round work 3 trebles in the first corner. In the next 3 corners (chain spaces) work 3 trebles, 2 chain and 3 trebles. In the last corner, where you started the round, work 3 trebles and 2 chain. Finish the round with 1 slip stitch in the top chain from the start of the round. When this round is completed you will have 8 groups of 3 trebles.

4. Work 3 trebles in the first corner. Work 3 trebles in the next space. Work 3 trebles, 2 chain and 3 trebles in the next corner. Continue working each side of the square and a corner until you reach the last corner. Work 3 trebles and 2 chain in the last corner. Finish the round. When this round is completed you will have 12 groups of 3 trebles.

5. From now on, simply continue outwards. For each round you add one more group of trebles on all 4 sides of the square. You decide for yourself when the blanket is finished and when and how you change colour as you go.

6. When you feel that your blanket is finished, cut the yarn and weave in the ends. Maybe it will never be finished and your blanket will end up being a never-ending project, just like mine did.

Start by making a row of chain and joining it into a ring, in which you work trebles.

Making the first corner of the square.

Work round the chain arch and in all the spaces.

Finish each round with a slip stitch in the third chain.

My mother's cushion

My mother first travelled to Greece with her family when she was a little girl, and has returned there again and again as an adult. The Mediterranean calls out to her. She comes home from every trip with seashells from various Greek beaches, and now they are all over her house. Over the years my mother has used them to decorate the breakfast table on our birthdays and made them into wind chimes that jingle when the summer breeze blows through the house, and she has also placed special shells in selected spots, to reminding her of the sparkling, turquoise sea and the velvety nights in Greece. I grew up surrounded by seashells and even as a child I was deeply inspired by all things maritime. That's why I designed this cushion for my mother, and she loves it because it takes her thoughts back to the sea and sunshine.

I also love this cushion – for its colours, its design and the entire process of making it. I can see it clearly in my mind's eye, lying on a chair in the corner of my mother's spiritual healing studio radiating good energy.

Size

50 × 50 cm – or the size of a cushion you have lying around at home and would like to cover.

Materials

- 100% cotton in DK weight
- 200 g colour A
- 100 g colour B
- 50 g colour C
- 50 g colour D

- 4.5 mm crochet hook

Tension

10 × 10 cm = 15 treble crochet in width and 8 rows in height.

If you have more stitches and rows to 10 × 10 cm,
change to a larger hook.

If you have fewer stitches and rows to 10 × 10 cm,
change to a smaller hook.

Worth knowing before you start

The cushion cover consists of two parts, worked from the bottom up and then crocheted together. Lastly, you make four tassels and sew one on each corner of the cushion.

Techniques

At the beginning of each row you start with a double crochet, work one chain, which functions as a turning chain. This stitch is not counted as a double crochet.

At the beginning of each row you work in double treble crochet, make 4 chain, which function as turning chains. These chains correspond to the first double treble of the row. You can read more about turning chains on pages 57-59.

My mother's cushion

The instructions given for the cushion cover here will fit a cushion measuring 50 × 50 cm. The cover can be made in any size, as long as the number of stitches in the first row of chain is a multiple of eight. When you have decided what size you want to make the cover and worked out the number of stitches you need, you must always add one extra chain, plus another to function as a turning chain.

1. With colour A, make a row of 64 chain + 1 extra chain + 1 more chain as a turning chain (66 chain in total).

2. Work 1 double crochet in the second chain from the hook and work a double crochet in each chain to the end of the row. You will end up with 65 double crochet.

3. Turn the work with 1 chain and work 1 double crochet in each stitch to the end of the row.

4. Repeat step 3 one more time.

5. Now work charts A.1 and A.2 alternately a total of 7 times vertically, changing colours as explained in step 6 below. See charts on page 115.

6. At every colour change, cut the yarn of the previous colour and join the new colour. Join the new colour as follows: begin the last stitch with the old colour, but change to the new colour the last time you pull the yarn through and complete the stitch. Tie the ends in a knot and leave them hanging (see pages 87–90 for more about changing colours). Change between colours B, C and D on each row of the shell pattern and use colour A for the rows of double crochet in between the shell patterns. Note that when working the double crochet rows in colour A you will need to work a double crochet between each two shells over the top of the chain linking the shells, into the double crochet stitch in colour A immediately below it.

7. Now work chart A.1 once, cut the yarn and weave in the ends.

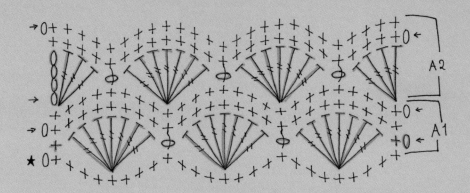

Key to chart

0 = Chain

+ = Double crochet

T = Double treble crochet

★ = This row has already been worked.
The chart therefore really starts with
the row above.

→ = Indicates where each row starts

⬭ = Double crochet between the two shells over
the top of the chain linking the shells, and
into the double crochet stitch in colour A
immediately below it

The pattern is worked by alternating rows of 'shells'...

... and rows of double crochet.

Make two identical pieces for the front and back of the cushion.

Crochet the two pieces together with half trebles to join all the seams of the cushion.

8. Now work the edging. As you do this, you can crochet over all the ends left hanging from the colour changes and thus avoid having to weave them in individually. Work the edging all the way round in double crochet in colour A. Work as follows: Start in one of the sides and work double crochet evenly spaced. At all the corners work 3 double crochet in the same corner stitch. When you reach the place where you started the edging, finish the round with a slip stitch in the first double crochet. Cut the yarn and weave in the ends.

9. Repeat steps 1–8 to make the second side of the cushion cover.

10. Now crochet the two parts of the cover together using colour A. Place the parts one on top of the other and join the first 3 sides with half trebles. You can place the parts together however you like, as there are no right or wrong sides. Replace the first half treble with 2 chain. Work 3 half trebles in each corner stitch.

11. Before you join up the fourth side, insert the cushion into the cover. Crochet the last side together in the same way as the other three and finish the round with 1 slip stitch in the topmost chain. Cut the yarn and weave in the ends.

12. Now make tassels for the corners in colour A. Work as follows: wind yarn around your four fingers until you reach your desired thickness for the tassel. Insert a strand between the yarn and your fingers, pull tight and tie a knot on top. Leave quite a long end hanging to use for sewing the tassel to the cushion cover. Remove the tassel from your fingers. Wind a strand of yarn around it several times about 1 cm from the top and weave in the end. Trim the ends of the tassel to the desired length. Repeat until you have four tassels.

13. Attach a tassel to each corner of the cushion cover, sewing into the corner with the strand of yarn from the tassel. Sew up and down until the tassel is firmly attached and weave in the ends.

Chequered lampshade

A crocheted lampshade. Lovely, isn't it? A friend once sent me a photo of a lady who had crocheted all kinds of covers for everything in her home – the sofa, chairs, tables and lampshades were all swathed in crochet. At the time my friend sent me this photo, I was extremely busy crocheting and had almost completely withdrawn from the world with my yarn and my hooks. She wrote: 'This is exactly like you right now.' When I saw that photo, I thought that the lady had taken things a bit too far. All the same, it must have inspired me, and that lady is undoubtedly responsible for the fact that I have now covered the first object in my home with crochet. The instructions below are based on free crocheting, not on a particular size of lampshade. Instead, I explain how to cover a lampshade that you may already have in your home. I'm a big fan of free crochet, because it means that you are at liberty to vary the size and shape yourself.

Size
To fit the lampshade that you want to cover.

Materials
- You can use any yarn you fancy, as long as it's quite thick – aim for an aran or chunky weight yarn (about 5 to 7mm thick). I used a wool mixture with recommended hook size 3.5 mm but I held two strands together to get the right thickness. I ended up using 200 g yarn for my lampshade.

- 4.0 mm crochet hook

Tension
10 × 10 cm = 14 trebles in width and 8 rows in height.

If you have more stitches and rows to 10 × 10 cm, change to a larger hook.

If you have fewer stitches and rows to 10 × 10 cm, change to a smaller hook.

Worth knowing before you start
Normally I wouldn't recommend reading the instructions all the way through before you start, as it can be more confusing than beneficial. However, in this case it's a good idea to read through the instructions before you begin crocheting. It will give you an overview of the project, which is good to have, as the instructions include free crocheting.

The lampshade is worked in trebles from the top down in a pattern that forms squares. You increase along the way, as the shade becomes wider lower down. You finish by working 2 rounds of double crochet at the bottom and 2 rounds of double crochet at the top. Work decreases in the last round of double crochet at the top as given in the final step.

Techniques

Each treble at the start of a round is replaced by 3 chain. Finish each round with a slip stitch in the third chain from the start of the round.

When you work in rounds in double crochet, make 1 chain at the beginning of the round. This chain doesn't count as a double crochet but it helps to make a neater start and end to the round.

When changing colours, start by working 1 stitch with the old colour, but don't make the last yarn over, leaving the stitch incomplete. Add the new colour and pull it through the loops on the hook. Continue by working the next stitch with the new colour. It is important to carry all the strands around inside the work so they are easy to pick up when you want to change colour again. You do this by crocheting over the colour you aren't using. This means the strand you're not using will be enclosed in the work and always near the hook when you want to go back to that colour (see pages 87–90 for more about working with colours).

Chequered lampshade

1. With your first colour, make a row of chain long enough to wrap around the top of your lampshade. The number of chain must be a multiple of 10 to ensure the chequer pattern will fit. I made 100 chain for my lampshade. If you want to begin each round with one colour chequer and end with the other colour you will need a multiple of 20 chain to give an even number of chequers. If you have an odd number of chequers then the first and last chequer of each row will be the same colour.

2. When you have made the right number of chain, work a slip stitch in the first chain to join the work into a ring.

3. No matter what size lampshade you have, work the first round with 1 treble in each chain. Start by making 3 chain (counts as the first treble) and work a further 9 trebles, so you have a total of 10 trebles in the first colour. Change to second colour at the tenth treble (see the techniques section on page 122 for more on how to change colour). Now

work 10 trebles in the new colour. Remember to work over the strand you aren't using so that it becomes hidden inside the work. Continue the round, alternating 10 trebles in one colour with 10 trebles in the other colour. Finish the round with a slip stitch in the third chain you worked at the beginning of the round.

4. After each round, pull the work down over the lampshade to estimate when you will need to work increases. If the work still fits the lampshade, continue repeating step 3 with 1 treble in each stitch in the same colour pattern.

5. Every time you have worked 5 rounds, whether or not they are increase rounds, change colour at the start of the sixth round, so you begin with the other colour, and change colour again at every tenth stitch. This creates the chequer pattern.

6. I worked 7 rounds without increases, because my lampshade doesn't get much wider at the bottom than it is at the top. On

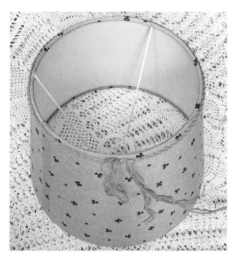

Make a row of chain long enough to wrap around the top of your lampshade.

When changing colour, remember to crochet over the yarn you are not using so it is hidden within the work.

Increase as you go so that your shade gets bigger.

Work an edging of double crochet to create a neat finish.

round 8 my work began to be tight around my lampshade and I increased as follows: *work 1 treble in each of the first 4 stitches (remember that the 3 chain at the start count as 1 treble), work 2 treble in the fifth stitch and 1 treble in each of the next 5 stitches.* Repeat from * to * to the end of the round. After this increase round there will be 1 more treble in each square, so you now work 11 trebles per square before changing colour. Remember, you can of course work the increase round before I did, if your lampshade gets wider sooner (see page 72 if you need some guidance on increasing).

7. After the increase round I worked 3 rounds of 1 treble in each stitch. Work as many rounds without increasing as you need to before your work becomes tight around your lampshade again.

8. When my work began to be tight around my lampshade again it was time for another increase round, which I worked as follows: *Work 1 treble in each of the first 5 stitches (remember that the 3 chain at the start count as 1 treble), work 2 trebles in the sixth stitch and 1 treble in each of the next 5 stitches.* Repeat from * to * to the end of the round. There are now 12 trebles per square in each colour.

9. After this round, I worked 2 rounds without increasing. I increased again in the last round of my lampshade, as the work was beginning to get tight around my lampshade again. I increased in this round as follows: *work 1 treble in each of the first 6 stitches (remember that the 3 chain at the start count as 1 treble), work 2 trebles in the seventh stitch and 1 treble in each of the next 5 stitches.* Repeat from * to * to the end of the round. There are now 13 trebles per square in each colour.

10. If your lampshade is bigger than mine, continue working rounds with and without increases as needed to get the correct fit. Each time you work a new increase row, remember to work 1 more treble before the increase than you did in the previous increase round. Also remember to follow the chequer pattern at all times, changing the colour sequence every sixth round.

11. When your work is big enough to cover your entire lampshade, work 2 rounds of double crochet in one of the colours at the bottom of the piece. Work as follows: *start the round by making 1 chain and work 1 double crochet in the stitch where you just worked one chain. Work 1 double crochet in each stitch to the end of the round. Finish the first round with 1 slip stitch in the first double crochet you worked.* Repeat from * to * one more time. Cut the yarn and weave in the ends.

12. Now work 2 rounds of double crochet at the top of the piece. Start the first round by inserting a strand of the same colour as you used for the bottom edge in between two of the trebles you worked at the start, because this round is worked between the stitches and not in each stitch. This gives a firmer round and a more attractive top edge. Work the top edge as follows: make 1 chain

and work 1 double crochet in the space where you just worked 1 chain. Work 1 double crochet in between all the trebles to the end of the round. Finish the first round with 1 slip stitch in the first double crochet you worked.

13. Now work a round of double crochet in the stitches of the previous round and decrease as follows: work 1 chain, then *work 1 double crochet in each of the first 8 stitches. Decrease by working the ninth and tenth stitches together.* (See page 68 for more about how to decrease in double crochet.) Repeat from * to * to the end of the round and finish the round with a slip stitch in the first double crochet you worked. Cut the yarn, weave in the ends and pull the work down over your lampshade.

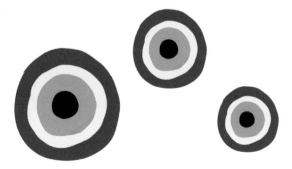

Plant basket

I've always loved plants and they have brought life into all the places I've lived for as long as I can remember. I'm not always very good at looking after houseplants and a couple of them have given up the ghost, but while they are alive, I do everything I can to give them a lovely home in the shape of a pretty pot cover.

When I moved away from home, the first thing I packed was a lovely Berber basket I had paid far too much money for. I had bought it specifically for my first flat, because Berber baskets are among the most beautiful things I have ever seen. Their lovely colours and patterns light up a room. Unfortunately, my basket disappeared during the move and I was left with my hands full of plants. Then I came up with the idea of combining two decorative items I'm especially fond of – Berber baskets and plant pot covers – and the idea of the plant basket was born. True Berber baskets are woven using a special technique that I dare not even attempt to try, so here is my crochet version of one of these baskets. I believe plants can sense when we show them love – and there's nothing more loving than a home you have crocheted just for them.

The baskets can be made in two different sizes, and you can of course use them to store all sorts of other things other than plants. If you choose to use them for plants, it's a good idea to line the basket with a plastic bag or to place a saucer or a plate in the bottom, so that water doesn't leak out into the basket when you water the plant.

Size
• Small basket
Base (diameter) – 14 cm
Height – 13 cm

• Large basket
Base (diameter) – 19 cm
Height – 19 cm

Materials
• 100% cotton in DK weight used double
Small basket: 100 g colour A – 50 g colour B – 50 g colour C
Large basket: 200 g colour A – 100 g colour B – 50 g colour C

• 4.5 mm crochet hook

Tension
10 × 10 cm = 14 half trebles in width and 9 rows in height.

If you have more stitches and rows to 10 × 10 cm,
change to a larger hook.

If you have fewer stitches and rows to 10 × 10 cm,
change to a smaller hook.

Worth knowing before you start
The plant basket is worked in rounds from the bottom up. You make
the base first and then work the patterned sides of the basket.

Techniques
The plant baskets are worked with the yarn held doubled to make
them thick enough to stand upright.

Each treble at the start of a round is replaced by 3 chain. When working with trebles, finish every round with 1 slip stitch in the third chain you worked at the beginning of the round. If you aren't sure about this, see page 62 for more about working in rounds.

Each half treble at the start of a round is replaced by 2 chain. When working with half trebles, finish every round with 1 slip stitch in the second chain you worked at the start of the round.

To create the pattern on the sides of the plant basket you will be changing colours. At the colour change, start by working 1 stitch with the old colour, but don't make the last yarn over and leave the stitch incomplete. Add the new colour and pull it through the loops on the hook. Continue by working the next stitch with the new colour. It is important to carry all the strands round inside the work so they are easy to pick up when you want to change colour again. You carry strands round the work by crocheting over the colours you aren't using, thus hiding the strands within the work (see pages 87–90 for more about working with colours).

Start by making a magic ring and working trebles into it.

The finished base of the plant basket.

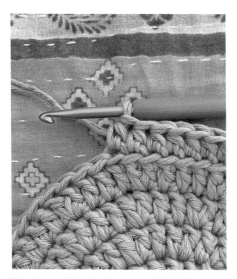

To shape the basket, work half trebles in the back loops.

Change colours according to the colour charts on page 137.

Instructions
Plant basket

1. Round 1: Working with double yarn in colour A, make a magic ring (see page 44 for more about making magic rings). Make 3 chain (which count as the first treble) and work a further 11 trebles in the ring so you have a total of 12 trebles. Close the round with 1 slip stitch in the third chain you worked at the beginning of the round.

2. Round 2: Work 2 trebles in each stitch, so that you have 24 trebles. It is a good idea to count the trebles on this round to make sure you have the correct number, as it's easy to accidentally work more stitches than you are supposed to. If you end up with too many stitches in the round, it will change the look of the whole basket.

3. Round 3: *Work 2 trebles in the first stitch and 1 treble in the next stitch.* Repeat from * to * to the end of the round, so you have 36 trebles.

4. Round 4: *Work 2 trebles in the first stitch and 1 treble in each of the next 2 stitches.* Repeat from * to * to the end of the round, so you have 48 trebles.

5. Round 5: *Work 2 trebles in the first stitch and 1 treble each of the next 3 stitches.* Repeat from * to * to the end of the round, so you have 60 trebles.

6. If you are making the small basket, you have now completed the increase rounds and can go straight to step 8.

7. If you are making the large basket, continue by working 2 rounds with 1 more treble between each increase, so you have 72 trebles after the first extra round and 84 trebles after the second extra round.

8. Whichever size of basket you are making, you now work 1 round of half trebles into the back loops only, to create the actual shape of the basket (see page 66 for more about working into the back loops). The first half treble is replaced by 2 chain and the round ends with 1 slip stitch in the second chain you worked at the beginning of the round. From now on, work only in half trebles. This will give the basket a denser structure and ensures it will not collapse.

9. You will now work the patterned rounds. If you are making the small basket, follow colour chart A opposite, working the chart 5 times per round. If you are making the large basket, follow colour chart B, working the chart 7 times per round (see page 78 if you aren't sure about how to read colour charts).

Colour charts
The starred line is the round you have already worked in the back loops, so start with the line above it. Every square in the chart corresponds to one half treble.

10. When you have worked to the top of the pattern the basket is finished and you can cut the yarn and weave in the ends. Note that even though there is no colour change in the last round of the pattern, it's a good idea to continue crocheting over the strands of the other colours. This will ensure that the last round of the basket maintains the same shape as the previous rounds. If you don't crochet over the other colours, the last round will be thinner than the previous ones and the difference will be clearly visible.

A

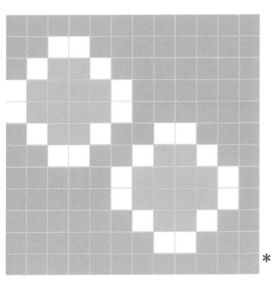

*

B

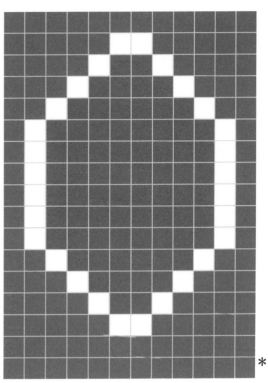

*

Pouffe

The pouffe is my dedication to independence. When young people move out of home, they're often on a very tight budget. And when you're setting up your new place, I know that it's possible to make do with a salvaged coffee table, a box full of yarn, a few beers and a lot of heart.

When I was about to fly the nest myself, I was absolutely determined that my first item of furniture would be a pouffe, so I set to work making one. I had a great time crocheting my own piece of furniture. The day I got the keys to my apartment, I set my finished pouffe down in the middle of the living-room floor and hung my photo of the singer and actress Jane Birkin on the wall. Then I sat there on my simple one-person seat with a smile on my face and started my adult life.

The pouffe is worked in T-shirt yarn, which is fun and a little bit different. The thick yarn means you will soon see results, so starting the pouffe isn't as scary as it looks. It took me three or four days to make mine.

Size
Base (diameter) – 38 cm
Height (approx.) – 18 cm

Materials
• T-shirt yarn
- 250 g colour A
- 250 g colour B
- 250 g colour C
- 250 g colour D
- 250 g colour E

• 6 mm crochet hook

• Cushions or other stuffing material

Tension
10 × 10 cm = 14 trebles in width and 8 rows in height.

If you have more stitches and rows to 10 × 10 cm,
change to a larger hook.

If you have fewer stitches and rows to 10 × 10 cm,
change to a smaller hook.

Worth knowing before you start
You make the top of the pouffe first, then the bottom and sides in
one. To finish, you fill it with cushions or stuffing and join the two
pieces together.

Techniques
Each treble at the beginning of a round is replaced by 3 chain.

Each round finishes with 1 slip stitch in the third chain you worked
at the beginning of the round.

You can make the pouffe in a single colour or with as many colour changes as you like. I don't give any guidance on changing colour in the instructions, as my own colour changes were done spontaneously. So if you decide to make a multicoloured pouffe, just change colours when it feels right. To do this, you need to first finish the round after which you want to switch to a new colour. Work a slip stitch in the third chain you made at the beginning of the round, then add the new colour and pull the strand of the colour of the previous round tightly round the new colour. If I already know that I don't want to use the colour from the previous round again, I cut the yarn, leaving an end of about 5 cm. You can work over the end of the old colour with the new colour to fasten it in. If you know that you will want to use that colour again, don't cut the yarn and instead carry it up along the work until you want to use it again.

If you aren't sure about how to change colours, it's a good idea to read about it on pages 87–90 before starting on the pouffe.

Instructions

Pouffe

Top

1. Round 1: Start by making a magic ring (see page 42). Make 3 chain, which count as the first treble, and work a further 11 trebles into the ring, so you have a total of 12 trebles. Finish the round with a slip stitch in the third chain you made at the beginning of the round (see page 62 if you aren't sure about how to work in rounds).

2. Round 2: Work 2 trebles in each stitch, so you have 24 trebles. It's a good idea to count the trebles to be sure you have the right number, 24, as it is easy to work more stitches than you should. If you end up with too many stitches in the round, it will change the look of the whole pouffe.

3. Round 3: *Work 2 trebles in the first stitch and 1 treble in the next stitch.* Repeat from * to * to the end of the round, so you have 36 trebles.

4. Round 4: *Work 2 trebles in the first stitch and 1 treble in each of the next 2 stitches.* Repeat from * to * to the end of the round, so you have 48 trebles.

5. Round 5: *Work 2 trebles in the first stitch and 1 treble in each of the next 3 stitches.* Repeat from * to * to the end of the round, so you have 60 trebles.

6. Continue working increase rounds until you have worked a total of 11 rounds. Continue increasing by working one more treble between each increase. You should have 132 trebles.

7. Round 12: *Work 1 treble in each of the first 10 stitches. Work 2 trebles in the next stitch.* Repeat from * to * to the end of the round, so you have 144 trebles.

8. Round 13: Work 1 treble in each stitch over the whole round.

9. Round 14: *Work 1 treble in each of the first 11 stitches. Work 2 trebles in the next stitch.* Repeat from * to * to the end of the round, so you have 156 trebles.

Start by making a magic ring, working trebles into it.

Work increase rounds to make the top of the pouffe bigger.

Increasing with trebles.

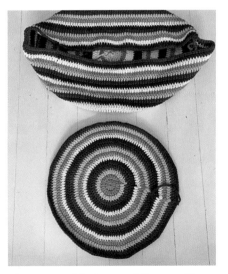

The top and bottom of the pouffe before assembly.

10. Round 15: Work this round in double crochet. Make 1 chain before working the first double crochet, as this will produce a neater start and end to the round. This chain doesn't count as a double crochet, so remember that the first double crochet should be worked into the same stitch as the chain. *Work 1 double crochet in each of the first 12 stitches. Work 2 double crochet in the next stitch.* Repeat from * to * to the end of the round, so you have 168 double crochet. When the round is complete, fasten off with 1 slip stitch in the first double crochet. Cut the yarn and weave in the ends.

The top of the pouffe is now finished and you will now make the bottom and sides in a single piece.

Bottom

1. Make the bottom of the pouffe by following steps 1–10 of the top, so you have 168 double crochet, but do not cut the yarn.

2. When you have completed steps 1–10, continue by making the sides. This means you will now work in rounds without increasing, as described below.

Sides

1. Round 1: Make 1 chain, and work 1 double crochet in each stitch to the end of the round. Remember that the first chain doesn't replace a double crochet. Finish the round with 1 slip stitch in the first double crochet.

2. Rounds 2–14: Work the next 13 rounds with 1 treble in each stitch. Remember that each treble at the start of a round is replaced by 3 chain, and every round finishes with 1 slip stitch in the third chain you worked at the beginning of the round.

3. Round 15: Make 1 chain and work 1 double crochet in each stitch to the end of the round. Finish the round with 1 slip stitch in the first double crochet. The side of the pouffe is now finished. Leave an end of about 2 metres before cutting the yarn, so that you can use it to sew the top of the pouffe to the sides.

4. Using a large darning needle and end of the yarn from the side of the pouffe, start sewing the 2 parts together. To do this, insert the needle through one stitch of the side and one stitch of the top, then draw the yarn through the 2 stitches and pull tight.

Continue in this way, but don't forget to stuff the pouffe before you finish closing the seam. I used three cushions for mine, but there are many other things you could use, such as old blankets or duvets. When the pouffe is well filled, sew up the remainder of the seam as shown above. Weave in the end and cut the yarn.

148

Accessories

I have a special place in my heart for crocheted accessories. And if I may say so myself, accessories are what I do best – I crocheted nothing else for a whole year. At one point, I designed a bag that proved extremely popular online and I had to work at lightning speed to keep up with demand.

What makes crochet accessories so appealing is that we can all make a little bit of our own personality shine through in these small items. I have always been very keen on creating things I could leave my own special mark on, and that's something I can really do with crochet bags and hats. When you have crocheted your first bag, hat or other accessory, you'll soon notice the special sense of freedom you get when you can simply put on a little crochet item that completes your outfit – whether you're off to a party, going travelling or just heading for a stroll around your neighbourhood. A crocheted accessory can quickly and easily breathe new life into your usual outfits. I promise you that at least one of the projects here will become your new best friend, the item that you always pick up when you're on your way out. These patterns are also great because they are relatively quick to complete.

My childhood bandana

When I was little, I always used to run around on the beach with my plastic sword, pretending to be a pirate. My obsession with pirates started when I saw the Disney version of *Peter Pan* for the first time. I discovered that the baddies had the coolest look, with all their gold jewellery and tattoos. One of the pirates had a bandana tied round his head – and I wanted to look like that. So the bandana became my new best friend, a bit of a costume I could wear every day without attracting too much attention and without anyone else having to join in the game. After I grew up, the bandana remained my best friend, though now for a different reason. It's my lifesaver on bad hair days. A bandana is easy to tie round your head when you're either too tired to do your hair or can't be bothered with it. This pattern is for a bandana with a more feminine look than the one I ran around in as a child. The instructions are beginner-friendly and the bandana is quick to make. I'm definitely going to be making more of them, because they also make perfect gifts.

Size
Width across long edge – 38 cm
Height – 19 cm

Materials
• 100% cotton in 4 ply weight
- 50 g colour A
- 50 g colour B

• 2.5 mm crochet hook

Tension
10 × 10 cm = 21 trebles in width and 12 rows in height.

If you have more stitches and rows to 10 × 10 cm,
change to a larger hook.

If you have fewer stitches and rows to 10 × 10 cm,
change to a smaller hook.

Worth knowing before you start
The bandana is worked in granny-square stripes from the middle
outwards and gets bigger with every row, because you increase
at both sides and in the middle. When you make these increases
the work becomes triangular in shape (see page 72 to read about
increasing).

Finish by adding an edge of double crochet, ties and a picot edging.

Techniques
The first treble and chain of each row are replaced by 4 chain,
which you use to turn the work (see pages 55–59 for more about
turning chains).

Make a row of chain, join it into a ring and work trebles and chain in the ring.

Work into the first chain arch, so the bandana gets wider every row.

Work the edge and tie in one.

Finish off with a picot edging.

Instructions
My childhood bandana

1. Make 4 chain with colour A and make 1 slip stitch in the first chain to form the row of chain into a ring. Make 4 chain that will count as the first treble and the first chain. Now work 3 trebles, 1 chain, 3 trebles, 1 chain and 1 treble into the ring you have just made. You can now continue by either following the chart on page 159 or by following the written instructions below beginning from step 2. Note that the chart shows only 9 rows. When it stops after the ninth row, continue working increases at each side, as established, until you have worked a total of 23 rows, and then continue from step 5.

2. Make 4 chain, which again correspond to the first treble and the first chain, and turn the work. Work 3 trebles and 1 chain in the first chain arch of the previous row. Work 3 trebles, 1 chain, 3 trebles and 1 chain in the next chain arch of the previous row. Work 3 trebles and 1 chain in the next chain arch of the previous row. Finish this row with 1 treble in the last treble of the previous row.

3. Make 4 chain, which again correspond to the first treble and the first chain, and turn the work. Work 3 trebles and 1 chain in the first chain arch of the previous row. Work 3 trebles and 1 chain in the next chain arch of the previous row. Work 3 trebles, 1 chain, 3 trebles and 1 chain in the next chain arch of the previous row. *Work 3 trebles and 1 chain in the next chain arch of the previous row.* Repeat from * to * once more. Finish this row with 1 treble in the last treble of the previous row.

4. Continue working in rows, working one more group of 3 trebles and 1 chain on each side of each row.

5. When you have worked a total of 23 rows (or more or fewer, depending on what size you want), cut the yarn and weave in the ends.

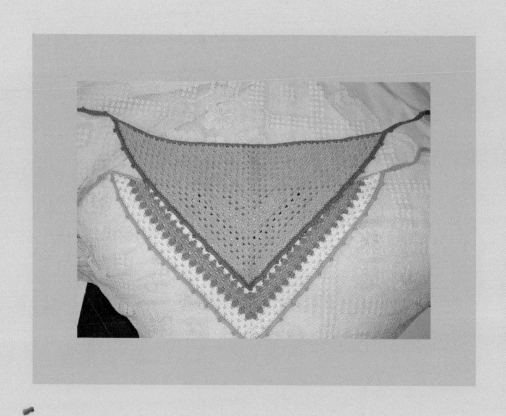

Border and ties

Now work a border in double crochet. When you reach the two corners at the bottom of the triangle, work chain, which will become the ties. Work the border and ties as follows:

1. Start by joining colour B at the corner where you have just ended with colour A (if you aren't sure how to do this, see page 89 for more about joining colours). Make 1 chain and work 1 double crochet in the first stitch of the previous row. Now work double crochet all the way up to the top corner and down to the other bottom corner. Work 1 double crochet in each stitch and each chain space. At the top corner work 3 double crochet in the chain space.

2. When you reach the bottom corner, make a row of 60 chain, which will form the first tie. When you have made the chain, work 1 double crochet in the second chain from the hook. Work 1 double crochet in each stitch to the end of the row of chain.

3. When you have worked your way back to the bandana itself, work double crochet along the bottom edge of the bandana until you reach the corner where you started the border. Here there are no clear stitches to work into, but do your best to work double crochet evenly spaced into the holes you can get at.

4. When you have reached the corner where you started, make the second tie. Work a row of 60 chain to match the one on the other side. Work 1 double crochet in the second chain from the hook and then 1 double crochet in each stitch to the end of the row of chain.

5. When you have got back to the bandana itself, work 1 slip stitch in the first double crochet of the edging. Cut the yarn and weave in the ends.

Picot edging

You finish the piece by making a picot edging. This type of edging creates delicate little points, known as picots, on the bandana. You work the picot edging from the end of one tie all the way around to the end of the other tie. Note that you don't work the picot edging along the bottom edge of the scarf. Work the picot edging as follows:

1. Start by joining colour B to the end of one tie. Work 1 chain, then work 1 double crochet in the first stitch. Work 1 double crochet in each of the next 7 stitches of the tie. You now have 8 double crochet and are about to make the first picot. If you want more picots on the bandana, work fewer double crochet in between them.

2. You make a picot as follows: Make 3 chain, insert the hook in the first chain and make 1 slip stitch.

3. Work 1 double crochet in the next 8 stitches and make another picot. Repeat until you reach the end of the second tie. When the edge is finished, cut the yarn and weave in the ends.

Start here

Key to chart

0 = *Chain*

Ŧ = *Treble*

Agnes's hat

The pattern for this hat is dedicated to my friend Agnes, the woman with a thousand hats. Since the earliest days of my adventures in crochet, I have wanted to crochet a hat for Agnes. But hats are difficult. Really difficult. There weren't many hat patterns I liked, so I decided to design one myself. Along the way I discovered just how difficult it is to work out the right increases and decreases to shape a hat that looks pretty and is comfortable to wear. So it's not surprising that developing this pattern involved a bit of trial and error.

I handed one hat after another over to Agnes, and the hats were good, but they weren't perfect. Nevertheless, Agnes wore them; and, what's more, she wore them with a smile on her face – a hat is a hat, after all. Meanwhile I struggled to crack the code and make this hat lover's eyes light up. Finally it happened: I cracked the code and found the right shape. So here it is, Agnes – here is the pattern for the perfect hat.

Size

Size 1: measures approx. 49.5 cm circumference
Size 2: measures approx. 58 cm circumference

Materials

• 100% cotton in DK weight
- size 1 – 100 g colour A, 50 g colour B
- size 2 – 150 g colour A, 50 g colour B

• 4.0 mm crochet hook

Tension

10 × 10 cm = 17 double crochet in width and 20 rows in height.

If you have more stitches and rows to 10 × 10 cm,
change to a larger hook.

If you have fewer stitches and rows to 10 × 10 cm,
change to a smaller hook.

Worth knowing before you start

The hat is worked in spiral rounds from the top down, with a colour
pattern halfway through.

Techniques

The hat is worked in double crochet in spiral rounds with colour
changes along the way. When working in a spiral, you insert a
stitch marker to mark the start and end of each round (see page 29
for more about how to use stitch markers). To shape the hat, you
increase and decrease as you go (see pages 68–72 for more on this).

Insert a marker at the start of the second round.

Join a new colour to work the pattern in the hat.

Change colour as you go along, following the colour chart on page 167.

Once the crown is complete it's time to start making the brim.

Instructions

Agnes's hat

1. Round 1: Make a magic ring (see page 44) in the main colour of the hat (colour A) and work 7 double crochet in the ring. Tighten the ring by pulling the loose end of the yarn.

2. Round 2: Work 1 double crochet in the first double crochet of the previous round and insert a stitch marker, which will mark the start of the first round. Remember to move the marker every time you start a new round. Work 1 more double crochet in the same stitch. Work 2 double crochet in each stitch all the way around to the stitch marker, so you have 14 double crochet.

3. Round 3: *Work 1 double crochet in the first stitch and 2 double crochet in the next stitch.* Repeat from * to * to the end of the round, so you have 21 double crochet.

4. Round 4: *Work 1 double crochet each of the first 2 stitches and 2 double crochet in the next stitch.* Repeat from * to * to the end of the round, so you have 28 double crochet.

5. Round 5: *Work 1 double crochet in each of the first 3 stitches and 2 double crochet in the next stitch.* Repeat from * to * to the end of the round, so you have 35 double crochet.

6. Round 6: * Work 1 double crochet in each of the first 4 stitches and 2 double crochet in the next stitch.* Repeat from * to * to the end of the round, so you have 42 double crochet.

7. Continue increasing, with 1 more double crochet between the increases on each round. If you are making size 1, work a total of 12 increase rounds, so you have 84 double crochet. If you are making size 2, work a total of 14 increase rounds, so you have 98 double crochet. Whichever size you are making, change to colour B in the last stitch of the final round. If you aren't sure about how to change colour, see pages 87-90.

8. Now continue by working the chart on page 167, repeating the chart 6 times around for size 1 – 7 times around for size 2 (see pages 75–78 for more about how to read a colour chart). Change to colour A in the last stitch of the final round of the chart in order to work the brim in the main colour of the hat.

Brim

When you have finished working the chart, make the brim in the main colour of the hat (colour A) as follows:

1. *Work 1 double crochet in each of the first 6 stitches and 2 double crochet in the next stitch.* Repeat from * to * to the end of the round, you have 96 double crochet (size 1) – 112 double crochet (size 2).

2. Work 2 rounds of 1 double crochet in each stitch. There are no increases in these rounds.

3. *Work 1 double crochet in each of the first 7 stitches and 2 double crochet in the next stitch.* Repeat from * to * to the end of the round, you have 108 double crochet (size 1) – 126 double crochet (size 2).

4. Work 3 round of 1 double crochet in each stitch. There are no increases in these rounds.

5. *Work 1 double crochet in each of the first 8 stitches and 2 double crochet in the next stitch.* Repeat from * to * to the end of the round, you have 120 double crochet (size 1) – 140 double crochet (size 2).

6. Work 1 round of 1 double crochet in each stitch. There are no increases in this round.

7. *Work 1 double crochet in each of the first 8 stitches and then make 1 decrease.* (See page 68 for more on decreasing in double crochet.) Repeat from * to * to the end of the round, you have 108 double crochet (size 1) – 126 double crochet (size 2).

8. Work 1 double crochet in each stitch on the last round.

9. When you have completed the last round, remove the stitch marker and work slip stitches over the next 2-3 stitches to make a neat ending. Cut the yarn and weave in the ends.

Colour chart

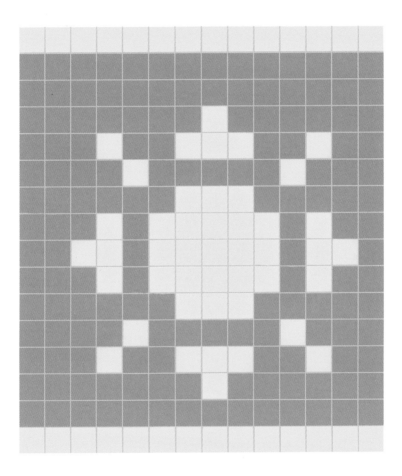

Crochet bikini

Whenever I sit crocheting in public, I encounter older ladies who get a special look in their eyes when they spot what I'm doing and say: 'Ooh, you're crocheting! I used to do that too, when I was young. Yes, we all went around in crocheted bikinis. They looked nice, but they weren't terribly practical.' I nod and agree with them. Crocheted bikinis get heavy as soon as they hit the water, so yes, they aren't very practical, but they are absolutely gorgeous. It must be amusing for the older generation to see young people being more or less consciously inspired by the fashions of their day. I had never seen a crochet bikini before I made my own, but I have since been told that they were all the rage on the beaches of Denmark when my grandmother was young. I can just imagine a 1970s beach full of beautiful women in colourful crochet cotton bikinis.

The first time I crocheted a bikini was on a warm and sunny September day. It was one of the last days of summer, and I was lying on the beach with my best friend. I worked as quickly as I could, because I wanted to be able to wear it just once before summer was completely over. I finished it, and that evening I wove in the yarn ends while we sat enjoying a cold beer. I was lucky, because I got up the next day to see one more warm late summer day. I quickly put on the bikini and, for what proved to be the last time that year, I cycled out into the sunshine and enjoyed the warmth – in my bikini.

Crochet bikinis send out a wonderfully cool vibe, which is probably the reason why they are so dear to my heart.

Size

The size of your favourite bikini. Try to find bikini bottoms that tie at the sides and a top consisting of two triangles joined with ties. That will make it easier to measure the size as you go along when making your bikini.

Materials

For the bikini you will need three colours (or as many colours as you fancy to make the bikini of your dreams), and you won't need very much yarn. This makes the bikini a perfect project for using up odds and ends of yarn. For the main colour (colour A) you will need about 100 g of cotton. For the other colours you won't need more than 50 g. Of course this is just an estimate, based on the amount I used to make my bikini. You may need more or less yarn than than I did.

- 100% cotton in 4 ply weight
- 100 g colour A
- 50 g colour B
- 50 g colour C

- 2.5 mm crochet hook

- Your favourite bikini to take your measurements from

Tension

10 × 10 cm = 21 trebles in width and 12 rows in height.

If you have more stitches and rows to 10 × 10 cm, change to a larger hook.

If you have fewer stitches and rows to 10 × 10 cm, change to a smaller hook.

Worth knowing before you start

You make the front of the bikini bottom first and then the back of the bikini bottom. Next you make the two cups of the bikini top in a zigzag pattern. Lastly you crochet the borders of the front and back of the bottom and the two cups of the top, followed by the ties for both the top and bottom.

Techniques

When you're working back and forth in rows, every treble at the beginning of a row is replaced by 3 chain, which you use to turn the work (see pages 57-59 for more about turning chains).

The bikini is worked with colour changes that create stripes. Don't cut the yarns when changing colours; leave them hanging until you come to use them again. Change colours at the end of each row by starting to work a stitch but not making the last yarn over, then bringing the new colour up the side of the work and finishing the stitch with the new colour. Work the next row with the new colour (see pages 87-90 for more about changing colours).

The instructions for this pattern include increases, so see page 72 if you aren't sure how to do this.

Instructions
Crochet bikini

Bottom

You make the bikini bottom by first working the front from the bottom up and then the back, also from the bottom up. Then you crochet a border around the front and back of the bikini bottom and work ties from each corner.

1. Lay the bottom of the bikini you want to use as a template out flat and make a row of chain in colour A that matches the width of the centre of the bikini bottom. When you have made the right number of chain, make 3 extra chain, which correspond to the first treble. Work 1 treble in the fourth chain from the hook and then 1 treble in each chain to the end of the row. When you reach the last treble of the row, join a new colour in the last yarn over of the stitch. Do not cut the yarn, leave it hanging (see pages 87–89 for more about adding a new colour. It's also described in the techniques section of the bikini pattern on page 171).

2. Now make 3 chain, which will function as a turning chain and count as the first treble. Work 1 treble in each stitch to the end of the row, but join a new colour in the yarn over of the last stitch. When you have joined in all three colours, each time you come to change colour, carry the new colour up the side of the work and continue working with it.

3. Continue working back and forth in rows of trebles. Each time you work a row, lay your work on top of the bikini bottom you are using as a template, so you can see where the bikini bottom starts to get wider. When your crochet bikini needs to get wider, work rows with increases on both sides. Work an increase row as follows: Make 3 chain (corresponding to the first treble) and work 1 treble in the same stitch. Work 1 treble in each stitch to 1 stitch before the end of the row, then work 2 trebles in the last stitch.
Continue working increase rows in this way until the front of your crochet bikini is the same size as the template bikini. Cut the yarns, leaving the ends hanging.

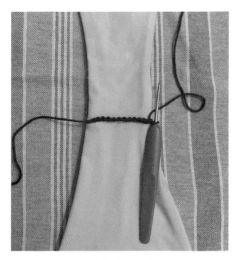

Make a row of chain as long as
the width of your template
bikini bottom.

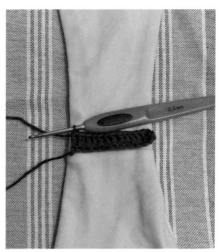

Work in trebles to the end of
the row.

Increasing at the beginning of
the row.

Work an edging of double crochet to
make a neat finish.

Work to match the bikini top you are using as a template.

Make crochet ties.

4. Now make the back of the bikini bottom. Start by joining a new colour to the opposite side of the row of chain you made at the start of the instructions. Make 3 chain (corresponding to the first treble) and work 1 treble in each stitch to the end of the row. Join a new colour in the last stitch.

5. Repeat step 3, where you work rows with 1 treble in each stitch. Continue until your template bikini bottom gets wider and you begin working increase rows. Increase in the same way as for the front. When you have reached the size you want for your bikini, cut the yarns, leaving the ends hanging.

6. Now work a border of double crochet all the way round the front and back of the bikini bottom. When you are working this border you can fasten in the ends you left hanging. Make sure you hold the ends close to the work and work double crochet over them so they end up inside the crochet border. Work the border as follows: join a new strand of yarn (colour A) and make 1 chain before working the first double crochet. Now work all the way round with 1 double crochet in each stitch. At the sides of the crocheted bottom there are no clear stitches to work into, so work double crochet wherever it makes sense, as evenly spaced as possible, otherwise the work may curl up. At each corner work 3 double crochet in the same corner stitch. When you're about to finish the first round of the border, work 1 slip stitch in the first stitch. Then work 1 chain and 1 double crochet in the same stitch and work a second round of border, this time with 1 double crochet in each stitch and 3 double crochet in each corner stitch. Cut the yarn and weave in the ends.

Top

The top is made up of 2 triangular pieces. You start by making the top of one triangle and then increase at the sides and in the middle to create a triangular shape. To finish the top, you work a double crochet border around each triangle and then make crochet ties at each corner. The second triangle is worked the same way.

1. Make 2 chain plus 3 extra chain that will function as turning chains. Work 1 treble in the fourth chain from the hook and 1 treble in the last chain, so you have a total of 3 trebles in the first row. Remember to change colour every row. Join the new colour in the last stitch.

2. Now work the first increase row. Make 3 chain (corresponding to the first treble), and work 1 treble in the same stitch. Work 3 double crochet in the next stitch (counts as 1 treble and 1 increase) and work 2 trebles in the last stitch. Remember to change colour in the last stitch.

3. Work the next 3 rows as established in Step 2 with 1 increase at each side, this time working 3 trebles in the central stitch. For the remaining stitches where you aren't working increases, work 1 treble in each stitch. The central treble increases form the zigzag pattern.

4. Now work one row, in which you increase only in the central stitch, not at the sides.

5. On the next row you again increase both at the sides and at the centre. Continue working alternate rows with and without increases at the sides, while always increasing at the centre. Lay your work on top of the bikini top you are using as a template and measure how big the cup needs to be. When the centre of the bottom of your work meets the bottom of your template you have finished working in rows. Your triangle may look quite wide, but that is intentional, as the bikini will stretch a bit vertically when you have worn it a couple of times.

6. The bottom line of your work will now come to a point and will need to be levelled off a little before you have completely finished with the first triangle. You do this as follows: Work 1 treble in each stitch until there are 4 stitches of the previous row remaining before the central stitch. Now work 1 double crochet in each of the next 9 stitches across the middle of the work. Then work 1 treble in each stitch to the end of the row.

7. Work the next row in the same way, but with 6 more double crochet across the centre section: Work 1 treble in each stitch until 7 stitches of the previous row remain before the central stitch. Work 1 double crochet in each of the next 15 stitches across the middle of the work. Work 1 treble in each stitch to the end of the row.

8. Work the last row in the same way, but with 6 more double crochet across the centre section: Work 1 treble in each stitch until 10 stitches of the previous row remain before the central stitch.

Work 1 double crochet in each of the next 21 stitches across the middle of the work. Work 1 treble in each stitch to the end of the row. Cut the yarns, leaving the ends hanging.

9. Now work a border of 2 rounds of double crochet around the triangle. Work the border in the same way as for step 6 of the bottom.

10. Work a second triangle for the bikini top by repeating steps 1-9.

Ties

Finish by making the ties coming from the 2 triangles of the bikini top and the corners of the bottom. The straps and ties are worked using a technique that produces a result resembling small seashells. It's the perfect look for a crochet bikini! Make the ties as follows:

1. Work the ties for the bikini top first. Take one of the triangle pieces and work a tie starting from its top. You do this as follows: Join a strand of yarn in colour A to the top of the triangle and make 3 chain. Then work 2 trebles together in the same stitch. Work as follows: *Wrap the yarn over the hook, insert the hook in the stitch where you worked 3 chain, pull the yarn through the stitch, yarn over and pull it through the first 2 loops.* Repeat from * to * one more time and then wrap the yarn over the hook and pull it through all the loops on the hook. Make 1 chain and then repeat from * to * 3 times in total and finish by wrapping the yarn over and pulling it through all the loops on the hook. Remember that all these stitches must be worked in the same stitch.

2. Turn the work and work 2 slip stitches over to the middle of the first 'seashell', so you can now make a second 'shell' around the chain arch (see page 67 for more about working around a chain arch). Make 3 chain and work 2 trebles in the chain arch, then work 1 chain and 3 trebles together in the chain arch. Work shell in chain arch as established in step 1.

3. Repeat step 2 until your tie is long enough to tie at the back of your neck.

4. Repeat steps 1–3 at all the corners of the triangles, but note that the 2 ties that join the cups together at the front will not be nearly as long as those to be tied across the back and at the back of the neck. I worked 15 'seashells' for the short ties and 35 'seashells' for the long ties.

5. Make ties for the bikini bottom by repeating steps 1-3. I have made versions of this bikini bottom with and without adjustable ties and I really recommend making adjustable ties, as the bikini will probably stretch slightly when it comes in contact with water.

6. When all the ties have been completed, weave in the ends and your bikini is finished.

The little bag that went viral

In December 2019 I crocheted a little chequered bag that swiftly went viral on social media. I was contacted by the YouTuber and influencer Emma Chamberlain, who had seen my bag and wanted to get her hands on one. I quickly made a chequered bag and sent it off to her. After she shared the bag on her channel, I was overwhelmed with orders, including one from the American dancer Maddie Ziegler, who also said she just had to have this little crochet item.

This sudden explosion of crochet as a fashion phenomenon left me speechless. When I first started to crochet, I did it in secret, because I thought it was a bit embarrassing. However, after having designed and made the little chequered bag, you can bet I was extremely proud of having crocheted a bag that so many people wanted. Many people have subsequently tried to recreate it and there are several tutorials on YouTube that show you how to make it. You can see photos of my original chequered bag on pages 190–191.

It's a really functional bag and that's why I've included a version of it in this book. The actual shape of the bag is the same as that of the chequered bag that went viral, but the pattern is different, as this one has vertical stripes. The stripes remind me of the lovely colourful awnings and parasols that often adorn cafés and small markets in southern European countries, and the stripes give the bag a lovely summery vibe.

Size

23 cm in width × 17 cm in height
The handle can be made any length you like.

Materials

- 100% cotton in DK weight
- 50 g colour A
- 100 g colour B
- 100 g colour C

- 3.0 mm crochet hook

Tension

10 × 10 cm = 22 trebles in width and 9 rows in height.

If you have more stitches and rows to 10 × 10 cm,
change to a larger hook.

If you have fewer stitches and rows to 10 × 10 cm,
change to a smaller hook.

Worth knowing before you start

You make the bottom of the bag first, working back and forth in
rows. Then you work the rest of the bag in rounds and finish with
a handle on each side which you sew together.

Techniques

Each treble at the beginning of a row or round is replaced by
3 chain.
When you work in rounds, each round finishes with 1 slip stitch in
the third chain you worked at the beginning of the round (see pages
62-63 for more about working in rounds).
There are a lot of colour changes in this item and you should carry
the strands you aren't using round inside the work (see pages
87-90 for more about joining new colours, changing colours and
how to carry colours not in use).

The little bag that went viral

Bottom

1. In colour A, make 49 chain plus 3 extra chain that function as the first treble.

2. Work 1 treble in the fourth chain from the hook, but don't pull the yarn through the final time, as you should join colour B here. Pull the strand of colour B through the stitch.

3. *Now work into the row of chain as follows: 6 trebles in colour B and 2 trebles in colour A. Now join colour C and work 6 trebles in colour C and 2 trebles in colour A.* Remember to crochet over the colours you aren't using so they are hidden inside the work.

4. Repeat from * to * twice more, so you have a total of 50 trebles after the first row.

5. Make 3 chain, that will function as the first treble in colour A, which is the colour you ended with after the first row, and turn the work. Now work a complete

row of trebles in the same colours as the previous row, so vertical stripes begin to form.

6. Continue in rows in this way until you have worked a total of 5 rows. The bottom of the bag is now complete and you're about to make the sides.

Sides

From here on, the bag is worked in rounds, so you no longer have to turn the work to start a new row. Remember that each round starts with 3 chain, which correspond to the first treble. You now make colour changes following the charts on page 188.

1. Work along one short edge of the bag bottom piece following chart A.1 (see page 78 if you aren't sure about working from colour charts). Work the trebles in the short edge of the bottom of the bag, beginning with a 3 chain to count as the first treble. Here there are no clear stitches to work into, so just do the best you can to work 10 stitches, evenly spaced.

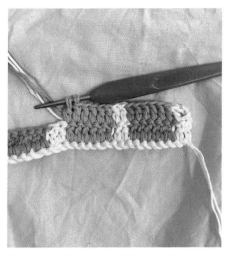

Change colour according to the chart on page 188.

Work into the short edge of the bottom of the bag.

Work into the back loops to create the shape of the bag.

When changing colours, remember to work over the strands you aren't using so they are hidden inside the work.

2. Work along the front of the bag following chart B.1. This part of the round is worked in the back loops only to create the shape of the bag (see page 66 for a description of how to crochet in the back loops). Work chart B.1 a total of 3 times, so that you've worked 48 trebles. Lastly work chart C.1 once, so that you've worked another 2 trebles and are at the end of the long side of the bag.

3. Work along the other short edge of the bag following chart A.2, so that you've worked 10 trebles. Work this edge in the same way as the first edge – see step 1.

4. Work along the back of the bag in the same way as the front, working in the back loops only. Work following chart B.2 a total of 3 times, so that you've worked 48 trebles. Lastly work chart C.1 once so that you've worked another 2 trebles and are at the end of the long side of the bag.

5. Finish the first round by working 1 slip stitch in the third chain you worked at the beginning of the round.

6. Continue working in rounds in trebles, with the same pattern and colour changes as for the previous round, but from now on, work into both loops, not into the back loops only. Remember to begin each round with 3 chain corresponding to the first treble.

7. When you have worked a total of 16 rounds, the main part of the bag is complete.

Handle

Work 2 handles – 1 on each side – and finish by sewing them together to make a single handle. There are decreases in the handles, so they get narrower with each row (see page 71 for how to decrease in trebles).

1. Start by working 1 treble in each of the 30 stitches of one side of the bag. Begin 10 stitches before the end of the long side, work the 10 stitches across the short side and then finish after the first 10 stitches of the next long side. Remember to follow the colour pattern of the bag, so the stitch you work will be the same colour as the stitch of the previous row you are working into.

2. Make 3 chain, corresponding to 1 treble. Turn the work and work 2 decreases one after the other. Work 1 treble in each stitch until 5 stitches remain. Work 2 decreases

The handle is shaped by working
decreases at each side.

and finish with 1 normal treble the in last stitch of the row. When you have worked the first decrease row, you will have 26 trebles.

3. Work 4 more rows with 2 decreases at each side, in the same way as in step 2, so you have 10 trebles. Remember to change colour, even though you are decreasing. The colour changes can be a bit tricky when you are decreasing and the decreases will not always perfectly match the colours of the previous row, but it doesn't matter too much, and will be almost invisible when the bag is finished. You change colour in the middle of a decrease by starting the decrease with the first colour. Before you continue the decrease into the next stitch, drop the strand you are working with, change to the new colour and complete the decrease.

4. When you have worked the 4 decrease rows, work the next 17 rows without decreasing. If you want to make the handle longer, continue working more rows. If you want a shorter handle, work fewer than 17 rows.

5. When you have finished one handle, cut the yarn and weave in the ends.

6. Make a second handle at the other side. Follow the colour pattern that applies to the second short edge of the bag as you did in step 1.

7. When you have finished the second handle, cut the yarn, and leaving an end of colour A about 30 cm long. Use this end to sew the 2 handles together. In this case I would recommend sewing them together with backstitch, which you can read about on page 94. Weave in the other loose ends remaining on the handle.

When you have made a handle on each side, you are ready to sew them together.

Pattern charts

Each square equals 1 treble.

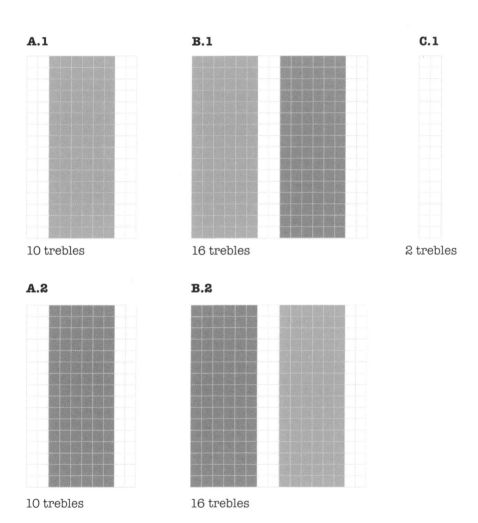

A.1

10 trebles

B.1

16 trebles

C.1

2 trebles

A.2

10 trebles

B.2

16 trebles

Raffia bag

Years ago I went on a holiday to Mexico that made such a deep impression on me that almost everything I crochet draws inspiration from that wonderful country. I was greatly inspired by the colours, the scenery, the animals and the little stalls selling jewellery and bags. I was only about eight years old at the time but all the same, when I close my eyes, I can remember the intense humid heat and the chalky-white, silky-soft sand between my toes.

Many of the women carried lovely woven basket bags and one day I want to go back to Mexico with this raffia bag over my shoulder. Of course it's crocheted, not woven, but the look of it reminds me of those basket bags. Personally, I think it's the best basket of all. It goes with all kinds of outfits, it's roomy and it's made of raffia – a fantastic material that is strong and water-repellent. This bag is perfect for the beach, as sand and water won't ruin it. Working with raffia can be a bit hard on your hands, but it's worth it all when you sling your lovely new bag over your shoulder and go out into the world – maybe even to Mexico.

Materials

- Raffia (I recommend the one made by Hobbii. Wool and the Gang also have some nice raffia yarns, but they are a bit thinner so would need to be used double for this pattern.)
- 300 g

- 6.0 mm crochet hook

Tension

10 × 10 cm = 11 trebles in width and 5 rows in height.

If you have more stitches and rows to 10 × 10 cm, change to a larger hook.

If you have fewer stitches and rows to 10 × 10 cm, change to a smaller hook.

Worth knowing before you start

The bottom of the bag is worked in double crochet from the centre outwards. The sides are worked from the bottom up, and lastly you make a handle on each side and sew them together.

Techniques

The bottom of the bag is worked in double crochet in spiral rounds. When you work in this way you insert a stitch marker mark where each round begins and ends (see page 29 if you have never used a stitch marker before or need to remind yourself how to use one). The sides are made with alternating rounds of double crochet, trebles and chain, which together create a hole pattern. Each time you start a round of double crochet that isn't part of the bottom of the bag, work 1 chain before the first double crochet. This makes a neater end to each round. Finish each round with 1 slip stitch in the first double crochet. Each time you work rounds of trebles and chain, replace the first treble and chain with 4 chain. Finish each round with 1 slip stitch in the third chain you worked at the start of the round (see pages 62–63 if you aren't sure about working in rounds).

When you make the handles, make 3 chain at the beginning of each row, which will replace the first treble and function as a turning chain (see pages 57–59 to read more about turning chains).

Instructions
Raffia bag

Bottom

1. Round 1: Start with a magic ring (see page 44) and work 7 double crochet in the ring. Tighten the ring by pulling the loose end of the yarn.

2. Round 2: Work 1 double crochet in the first stitch of the previous round and insert a stitch marker to mark the beginning of the first round. Remember to move the marker each time you begin a new round. Work 1 more double crochet in the same stitch. Work 2 double crochet in each stitch of the round until you reach the marker, so you have 14 double crochet.

3. Round 3: Continuing to move the stitch marker as established, *work 1 double crochet in the first stitch and 2 double crochet in the next stitch.* Repeat from * to * to the end of the round, so you have 21 double crochet.

4. Round 4: *Work 1 double crochet in each of the first 2 stitches and 2 double crochet in the next stitch.* Repeat from

* to * to the end of the round, so you have 28 double crochet.

5. Round 5: *Work 1 double crochet in each of the first 3 stitches and 2 double crochet in the next stitch.* Repeat from * to * to the end of the round, so you have 35 double crochet.

6. Round 6: * Work 1 double crochet in each of the first 4 stitches and 2 double crochet in the next stitch.* Repeat from * to * to the end of the round, so you have 42 double crochet.

7. Continue increasing in this way, working 1 more double crochet between each increase on every round. Continue until you have worked a total of 12 increase rounds. You should have 84 double crochet.

8. Remove the stitch marker and work 1 slip stitch in the stitch where the marker was.

9. Work 6 rounds with 1 double crochet in each stitch, without increasing. Remember that each

Insert a stitch marker at the beginning of the second round.

Work increase rounds, so the bottom of the bag gets bigger.

Work alternate trebles and chain to create the hole pattern.

Work rounds of trebles in the hole pattern of the previous round.

round must begin with 1 chain. This chain does NOT count as a double crochet. Finish every round with 1 slip stitch in the first double crochet.

10. Now work 2 rounds of the hole pattern. Work the hole pattern as follows: Start by making 4 chain, which count as the first treble and chain. Skip 1 stitch, and work 1 treble in the next stitch. Make 1 chain and skip 1 stitch before working 1 treble in the next stitch. Continue working the hole pattern in this way to the end of the round, always skipping 1 stitch by working 1 chain after each treble. Finish the round by working 1 slip stitch in the third chain you worked at the beginning of the round. Work 1 more round of hole pattern in the same way, so you have a total of 2 rounds of holes.

11. Repeat steps 9 and 10 twice more.

12. Work step 9 once more.

13. Now make the first part of the handle. Work 3 chain, corresponding to the first treble. Work 1 more treble in each of the next 19 stitches, so you have a total of 20 trebles.

14. Make 3 chain, corresponding to 1 treble. Turn the work and work 2 decreases, one after the other (see page 71 for more on decreasing in trebles). Work 1 treble in each of the next 10 stitches and then work 2 decreases again. Finish the row with 1 treble in the last stitch. You should have 16 trebles.

15. Repeat step 14, so you end with 12 trebles after all the decreases. This time you will only have 6 trebles between the 2 decreases at each side.

16. Repeat step 14, so you end with 8 trebles after all the decreases. This time you will only have 2 trebles between the 2 decreases at each side.

17. Make 3 chain, turn the work and this time work just 1 decrease, 2 trebles, 1 decrease and 1 treble in the last stitch, so you have 6 trebles.

18. Now work the handle in rows with 1 treble in each stitch until it has reached the desired length. I ended up working 17 rows without decreases.

19. Cut the yarn, leaving a short end for sewing up the handle.

20. Work a second handle on the side exactly opposite by repeating steps 13–19.

21. Now join the 2 parts of the handle together, using the end hanging from one of them and sewing backwards and forwards. If desired, use backstitch (see page 94 for how to do this). Weave in the end and cut the yarn.

22. End by working a border on each side of the opening and handle of the bag. This gives the handle a nice finish. Start from the centre of the last round of double crochet you worked before you began making the handles. Work double crochet evenly spaced all the way up one side of the handle and all the way down until you are back where you started working the border. Make 1 slip stitch in the first double crochet of the border. Cut the yarn and weave in the ends.

23. Repeat step 22 on the other side of the handle.

The handle is shaped by working decreases at each side.

Finish by working a border of double crochet around the handles.

Clothes

Maybe you've already cottoned on, but I'm often a bit shy and can get butterflies in my stomach just thinking about having to go out into the real world without having my yarn and crochet hook to hide behind, because that's when I feel safest. One day I was invited to a big party in the real world with lots of people I didn't know. Two days before the party I started thinking about what I was going to wear. Whenever I feel a bit insecure, I get dressed up, because then at least I'll have a crazy outfit to hide behind when I don't have my crochet things with me. At that time, I had mainly crocheted accessories and I hadn't tried my hand at making clothes yet. But two days before this party, I decided to launch myself into crocheting my first sweater.

I succeeded, but I didn't sleep for the two days and nights leading up to that party. After all, you don't usually make a crochet sweater in such a short time. A quarter of an hour before I was due to leave the house, I worked the last stitch, wove in the ends and swiftly pulled the sweater over my head. As I cycled to the party, I felt that I had made something magical with this sweater and by the time I arrived, all my nervousness had disappeared. If you haven't tried wearing something you have crocheted yourself yet, maybe you don't know this feeling, but to me it seems as if the crochet item works like a piece of armour when I put it on. I realized I felt more self-assured wearing that sweater than I had ever felt before. Maybe it was because with every stitch, a little self-love and a touch of self-assurance were woven in with the yarn. Ever since that day, I have always gone out wearing something crocheted when I have to do something that requires a little extra courage.

Odds and ends sweater

This sweater is a revolt against my inner perfectionist. That's because it is the only pattern in the book where you can't control exactly what the result will be like. The trick is to lean back, start crocheting and look forward to seeing what you end up with. This sweater is definitely the crochet project in this book that I wear most often myself and it makes me feel good inside. Maybe this sweater is trying to teach me something? That sometimes it's OK to let go and see where that takes me? Maybe it won't go exactly as you wanted or expected, but nevertheless you will end up with a unique masterpiece.

You could probably call this sweater a kind of assistant for tidying up your balls of yarn, because before you start crocheting, you have to gather all the little odd ends or half-finished balls of yarn that are just lying around, taking up space. I actually unravelled an old knitted sweater of mine that was just gathering dust so that I was able to give the yarn from this old sweater new life by combining it with other little odds and ends of yarn I had lying around and using it to crochet my odds and ends sweater.

Size

The same size as your favourite sweater.

Materials

- Leftover yarn. I used about 650 grams.

- 4.5 mm crochet hook or whatever hook you fancy to get the right thickness for your sweater. My sweater ended up having a pretty dense fabric, because I decided to use a very small hook for the yarn I had lying around.

- Your favourite slightly oversized sweater.

Tension

There is no point in making a tension swatch, because there is so much freedom in the pattern and you don't need to achieve the same tension I did. However, I do recommend working a few rows of stitches with different hook sizes to see what kind of thickness you prefer for your sweater. You can use different weights of yarn in this sweater, but you will get a more even result if you mostly use the same thickness of yarn.

Worth knowing before you start

The sweater consists of 4 parts: a front and a back that you join together before working the 2 sleeves directly on them.

Techniques

When working back and forth in rows, each treble at the beginning of a row must be replaced by 3 chain, which are used for turning the work (see pages 57–59 for more about turning chains). When you work the sleeves and the neck border, you work in rounds and replace each treble at the start of a round with 3 chain. Finish every round of trebles with 1 slip stitch in the third chain you worked at the beginning of the round.

Instructions

Odds and ends sweater

Yarn

1. This sweater is made of lots of different yarns, so you need to get all your materials ready before you start crocheting. My sweater combines yarn from an old knitted sweater that I unravelled and remainders from previous projects, where I just had a metre or two of yarn left. But it doesn't have to be leftover yarn, you can of course use any yarn for this sweater – yarn you have had for ages and have never got round to using, or completely new yarn you have just been out and bought.

2. Start by making your own homemade ball of yarn. Whichever yarns you are using, cut strands of different lengths and knot each one together with a strand of a different colour, leaving ends of about 5 cm hanging from every knot. The lengths of the strands and the colours and thicknesses you combine are entirely up to you. There is no right or wrong way to do things, just wind up the strands as you go along and continue in this way until you have made your own ball of yarn. Now you're ready to start crocheting. Make the next ball in the same way when you have used up the first one.

Front

1. The first part you make is the front of the sweater. Start by measuring along the bottom of a slightly oversized sweater that you own and like the shape of. Using this measurement, make a row of chain the same length as the bottom of your sweater, andthen add an additional 2–4 chain to give you enough space to be able to sew the front and back together without the sweater becoming too tight. It's a good idea to make a note of the number of chain you cast on, as you will be casting on the same number of stitches for the back.

2. Work 3 chain, which count as the first treble, and work 1 treble in the fourth chain from the hook. Work 1 treble in each stitch to the end of the row. When you come to a knot with a colour change in your yarn, work past it so it will hang out of the work.

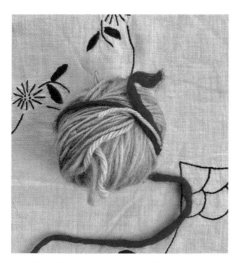

Cut lengths of yarn, tie them together and wind them into a ball.

Whenever you come to a knot, carry on crocheting. Make sure that all the knots stick out on the same side.

Work rounds of trebles to make the sleeve.

Work rounds of trebles to make the neck border.

3. When you have worked the last treble of the first chain, make 3 chain, turn the work and work one treble in each stitch to the end of the row. Remember to leave the colour-change knots hanging out of the same side of the work.

4. Continue working back and forth in rows of trebles until the front is the same length as your favourite sweater. You can also decide to make it a completely different length, it's entirely up to you. I chose to make mine shorter than the sweater I used as a template. When you reach the desired length, cut the yarn weave in beginning and ending yarn tails.

Back

1. The back is made in exactly the same way as the front. Start with a row of chain with the same number of chain as you made for the front. Work 1 treble in the fourth chain from the hook and work 1 treble in each stitch to the end of the row. Work back and forth in rows until you have the same number of rows as for the front. Cut the yarn and weave in beginning and ending yarn tails.

Joining up

1. Join the front and back together. Before you start, measure the size of the neck opening of the sweater you are using as a template. Measure the sweater when it's lying flat. Also measure down from the shoulder for the armhole. Note down the measurements.

2. Place the front and back with the right sides together, so the sides with the hanging ends are against one another. Join the shoulder seam, starting from one top corner. I use double crochet to join the seams (see page 93), but it's up to you to choose which method to use.

3. Mark the sides of the neck opening, perhaps with a stitch marker, and join the seam from the end of one shoulder to the first marker. Cut the yarn and weave in beginning and ending yarn tails. Join the shoulder seam from the opposite end to the other marker. Cut the yarn andweave in beginning and ending yarn tails.

4. Now join the seam from the bottom corner of the sweater up to the bottom of the armhole. Cut the yarn, weave in beginning and ending yarn tails and repeat on the other side. Turn the sweater right side out.

Sleeves

1. Now make the sleeves. Start by joining a new strand of yarn with a slip knot at the bottom of the armhole (see page 89 for more on how to join a new strand with a slip knot).

2. Make 3 chain, which count as the first treble, and work trebles all the way round the armhole. There are no clear stitches to work into, so work trebles evenly spaced round the armhole. I worked 1-2 trebles in each treble where I could find space. The more trebles you work in the first round, the wider your sleeves will be. Finish the first round of the sleeve by working a slip stitch in the top chain you worked at the beginning of the round.

3. You now have the start of the sleeve. Work the remainder of the sleeve in rounds of 1 treble in each stitch. Remember to start each round with 3 chain and finish with 1 slip stitch in the top chain.

4. Continue working in rounds as described in step 3. Try on the sweater as you go and work until you feel you have the perfect sleeve length for you. Cut the yarn and weave in beginning and ending yarn tails.

5. Make a second sleeve at the other side of the sweater by repeating steps 1-4.

Neck border

Finish by working a border around the neck opening.

1. Start by joining a new strand of yarn anywhere along the neck opening.

2. Make 3 chain, corresponding to the first treble, and work 1 treble in each stitch all the way round. Finish the first round with 1 slip stitch in the third chain you made at the beginning of the round.

3. Work as many rounds as you think you need, until the neck border is the height you want. I ended up working 3 rounds. Cut the yarn and weave in beginning and ending yarn tails.

The sweater is finished and you can leave it as it is, with the ends of the knots dangling, or you can use a large needle to weave in some of the ends until you're happy with the look of your sweater.

Pussycat's top

I want to wear this top at a festival, but it has to be a festival where we can turn back time and end up in the mid-1970s. I'm certainly not old enough to have experienced that crazy decade myself, but both my parents were born in the '70s and I have spent many a Sunday swooning over their childhood photos. Clothes were so unique and different back then. Fortunately, various outfits can almost take us on a journey back through time to that era. Crochet was a big thing when my parents were kids and that may be the reason why this craft is so close to my heart. No matter what I'm working on, I feel it has a vintage look about it. When I look at photos of festivals from the 1970s, I can see myself there in this top, with a pair of denim shorts and well-worn, dark brown cowboy boots.

Maybe you've already noticed that I get a lot of inspiration for my crochet from travel and films – especially films. This top is a tribute to Pussycat from Quentin Tarantino's *Once Upon a Time in Hollywood*, as in most of the scenes she wears a gorgeous backless rainbow-coloured crochet top. When I saw this movie, I knew I had to create my own version of that top – and here it is.

Size

The sizes of the top are measured along the bottom edges from corner to corner. To find the right size for your top you could hold a square scarf with roughly the same measurements as those given below against your body like a top and see how well it would fit you. You could also cut a square of fabric with the same measurements as the top and use it to get an idea of what size would suit you best. That's what I did. It's great to see the shape of the project in front of you before you get started.

XS – 28 × 28 cm
S – 36 × 36 cm
M – 43 × 43 cm
L – 51 × 51 cm

Materials

- 100% cotton in 4 ply weight
- 50 g colour A
- 50 g colour B
- 50 g colour C
- 50 g colour D
- 50 g colour E
- 50 g colour F

- 2.5 mm crochet hook for the main parts of the top
- 3.0 mm crochet hook for the ties

Tension

10 × 10 cm = 21 trebles in width and 12 rows in height on 2.5 mm hook.

If you have more stitches and rows to 10 × 10 cm, change to a larger hook.

If you have fewer stitches and rows to 10 × 10 cm, change to a smaller hook.

Worth knowing before you start

The middle part of the top is worked in rounds, starting from the centre. The outer part of the top is worked back and forth in rows. This helps to make the neck opening. Lastly you make ties of rows of chain at the top two 'corners' for the neckline and the two side corners, leaving the centre front lower corner without a tie.

Techniques

Each treble at the start of a round should be replaced by 3 chain. Every round of trebles ends with 1 slip stitch in the third chain you worked at the beginning of the round (see page 62 for more on working in rounds).

You can make the top in a single colour or change colour on each round. If you want a plain-coloured top, don't cut the yarn and continue working in the same colour.

If you want to use several colours, for every colour change you should complete the round and join a new colour. I leave an end of about 5 cm of the yarn I'm cutting off, start the new yarn, knot the 2 ends together and work the first 3-6 stitches of the next round or row over the ends. After that you cut off the ends, which have thus been fastened off. You can also join the new colour using a slip knot and again working over the non-working end from the previous round. You can read more about all this on pages 87–90, where you can find out about different methods for changing colour and pick the one that works best for you.

When working back and forth in rows, the treble at the start of each row should be replaced by 3 chain, which are used for turning the work (see pages 57–59 for more about turning chains).

Pussycat's top

1. Using smaller hook and colour A, start by working the centre of the top following chart A.1. Read the chart on page 222 as follows: Make 8 chain in colour A. Join the stitches into a ring by working 1 slip stitch in the first chain. Make 3 chain, which count as the first treble, then work a further 15 trebles in the ring. Finish the round with 1 slip stich in the third chain you worked at the beginning of the round. When the first round is complete you have a total of 16 trebles. Change to colour B.

2. Make 5 chain, which count as 1 treble and 2 chain. *Work 1 treble in the next stitch and 2 chain.* Repeat from * to * to the end of the round. Finish the round with 1 slip stitch in the third chain you worked at the beginning of the round. Change to colour C, which is joined in the chain arch, not in the treble you have just completed (see page 67 for more about chain arches).

3. With colour C, make 3 chain, corresponding to the first treble. Work a further 2 trebles around

the chain arch and make 1 chain. *Work 3 trebles around the next chain arch and make 1 chain.* Repeat from * to * to the end of the round. Change to colour D, which is joined in the chain arch, not in the treble you have just completed.

4. With colour D: *work 3 chain and 1 double crochet in the next chain arch. Do this twice more. Make 6 chain, which form a corner, so the square takes shape. Work 1 double crochet in the chain arch where you just worked 1 double crochet. Make 3 chain and 1 double crochet in the next chain arch.* Repeat from * to * to the end of the round. Finish the round with 1 slip stitch in the first chain you worked at the beginning of the round.

5. Make 3 chain, corresponding to the first treble, and work 2 more trebles in the first chain arch. Work 3 trebles in each of the next 2 chain arches. In the chain arch at the corner, work 5 trebles, 3 chain and 5 trebles. Work 3 trebles in the next chain arch. *Work 3 trebles in each of the next 3 chain arches. Work the next corner in the same

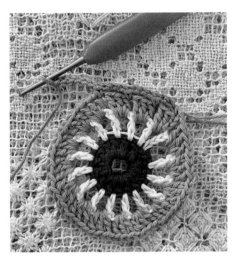

Start by working the centre of the top.

When the centre of the top is complete, continue working one treble in each stitch.

Shape the neckline by working back and forth in rows.

Change colour by joining in a new shade before starting a new row.

way as before with 5 trebles, 3 chain and 5 trebles. Work 3 trebles in the next chain arch.* Repeat from * to * to the end of the round. Finish the round with 1 slip stitch in the third chain you worked at the beginning of the round.

6. The centre of Pussycat's top is now complete. From now on you work rounds of 1 treble in each stitch and in each corner you work 2 trebles, 2 chain and 2 trebles in the chain arch. At the beginning of each round the first treble is replaced by 3 chain. Each round finishes with 1 slip stitch in the third chain you worked at the beginning of the round. Change colour as you go, if you want to. On my top I worked 2 rounds with colour B, 3 rounds with colour E and 3 rounds with colour F. When you have worked a total of 8 (size XS) – 12 (size S) – 16 (size M) – 20 (size L) additional rounds, work back and forth in rows along the square as given in step 7 below – so you are no longer working in rounds as before. These rows create the neckline.

7. Start the first row at the corner where you just finished the round. Join colour B in the first treble after the 2 chain. Work 3 chain, corresponding to the first treble, and work 1 treble in each stitch as far as the first corner. From here you work 3 trebles in the chain arch at the corner. Continue with 1 treble in each stitch along the sides and 3 trebles in the chain arches at the corners. Work until you reach the corner where you began the row, but don't work as far as the first treble you worked. Also, don't work the 2 chain of the previous round between the first treble of this row and the last treble you work in this row.

8. Make 1 chain as a turning chain and turn the work. Work 1 slip stitch in each of the first 3 stitches. Make 3 chain, which count as the first treble of the row. Work to the end of the row with 1 treble in each stitch and 3 trebles in the central stitch of each corner. Work the last treble in the third stitch from the end of the row, so you don't work into the last 2 stitches of the previous row.

9. Repeat the whole of step 8 another 4 more times. Change colour as you go, if you want to. Cut the yarn after the last row, and weave in the ends.

Neck border

1. Start at one side of the neck edge by joining the same colour you used for the last round you worked. Make 1 chain and work 1 row of double crochet across the neck edge. There are no clear stitches to work into, so work double crochet in suitable places, trying to space them evenly at the same time. I worked 1-2 double crochet in each treble. Take care not to work too many double crochet, otherwise the edge will curl up. When you have worked across to the other corner, turn the work with 1 chain and work 1 double crochet in each stitch to the end of the row. Cut the yarn and weave in the ends.

Ties

1. Now make a total of 4 ties, 1 from each corner of the neck edge and 1 from each corner of the sides of the top. Use the yarn double and start by joining it in the first corner with a slip knot (see page 89 for how to join yarn with a slip knot). Using a 3.0 mm hook, make a long row of chain. When your tie measures 50 cm, or your desired length, cut the yarn, fasten off the chain and tie a knot. Repeat this step in the other 3 corners.

Work across the side of the top to make a neat neck border.

Make the ties.

Key to chart

O = Chain

+ = Double crochet

⊤ = Treble

Beach
skirt

I have always admired my grandmother's crochet, and my great-grandmother's. They made all kinds of things with the most beautiful lacy patterns making different figures and shapes. You have probably come across lovely crochet lace, perhaps if you have travelled abroad and visited markets selling tablecloths, curtains and dresses with a lacy look. This lace pattern requires practice, but it's simple and fun to work once you've got the hang of it. I've always wanted to learn how to master the lace technique, as I find the look of this pattern extremely attractive. But many of the available lace patterns have a look that is more old-fashioned than I would like for my own crochet, which is why I decided to design the beach skirt. It's a perfect introduction to the lace technique, as you work all the way round in the same pattern. This makes the instructions easy to understand, and you will soon get used to working a pattern with holes in it. This skirt is nice to wear over a bikini when you're on the beach, but you can also make a longer version to wear when you go out at night and want a more dressed-up look.

Size

The size is based on your hip circumference at the widest point, so measure that and estimate which size will be best for you.

As you work there will be guidance on how to make the exact length you fancy. If you want to make a long skirt, I recommend making it a size larger, so it won't be too tight around your legs. This skirt has a drawstring, so the waist is adjustable.

XS – 80 cm hip circumference
S/M – 95 cm hip circumference
M/L – 110 cm hip circumference

Materials

• 100 % cotton in DK weight
- size XS – 250 g
- size S/M – 300 g
- size M/L – 350 g

• 3.5 mm crochet hook for the skirt
• 4.0 mm crochet hook for the tie

Tension

10 × 10 cm = 16 trebles in width and 10 rows in height
with 3.5 mm hook.

If you have more stitches and rows to 10 × 10 cm,
change to a larger hook.

If you have fewer stitches and rows to 10 × 10 cm,
change to a smaller hook.

Worth knowing before you start

The skirt is worked in lace pattern in rounds from the bottom up. Finish by inserting a tie at the waist.

Techniques

Each treble at the beginning of a round is replaced by 3 chain. Finish every round with 1 slip stitch in the third chain you worked at the beginning of the round.

Instructions
Beach skirt

1. Make 150 (size XS) – 175 (size S/M) – 200 (size M/L) chain and work 1 slip stitch in the first chain to close the work into a ring.

2. Make 3 chain, which form the first treble, work 1 treble in each chain to the end of the round and complete the round (see page 62 for more about working in rounds).

3. When you have completed the first round you will have 150 – 175 – 200 trebles. It's a good idea to count the number of stitches as you go along, as it's important to have the right number of trebles, otherwise the pattern will not work out correctly.

4. From now on work the pattern as follows: Work chart A.1 (page 232) a total of 6 (size XS) – 7 (size S/M) – 8 size M/L) times all the way round (see pages 75–77 for more about reading charts).

5. Now work the whole of chart A.2 (page 232) a total of 3 times vertically. If you want the skirt to be longer, continue working chart A.2 vertically. Remember that

this version is very short, as it is intended to be a little skirt you can wear over your bikini.

6. When you have reached the desired length for your skirt, work 1 round of trebles with decreases. Work this round in the front loops only (see page 66 if you aren't sure about this technique). Work the round of trebles in the front loops as follows: work 3 chain, corresponding to 1 treble. Work a further 8 trebles, so you have 9 in total. *Skip 1 loop and work 1 treble in each of the next 9 front loops.* Repeat from * to * until the round is complete. For size S/M, work 1 stitch in each of the last 5 stitches.

7. Work 4 rounds of 1 treble in each stitch, working in both loops as normal.

8. Finish by folding the rounds of trebles you have just worked over to the wrong side and crochet in place on the round you worked during step 6 to make a nice edge. Work as follows: Work 1 double crochet, inserting the hook in the

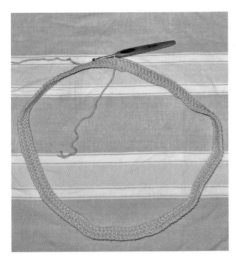

Make a long row of chain, join in a ring and work 1 treble in each chain.

Make the lace pattern by following the chart on page 232.

Fold the top round of trebles down to the round worked on step 6 and join together with double crochet.

Pull your chain through the skirt.

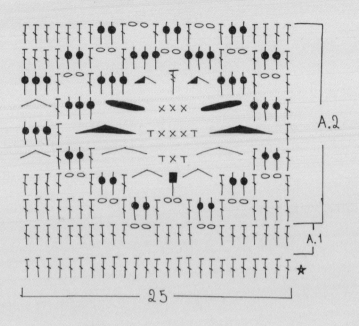

A.2

A.1

25

★ = This row has already been worked

○ = Chain

◢ = 4 chain

⌃ = 5 chain

⬬ = 6 chain

◢◣ = 7 chain

× = Double crochet in stitch

T = Double crochet in chain arch

Ŧ = Treble in stitch

♦ = Treble in chain arch

Ŧ = Double treble in stitch

⬛ = Double treble in chain arch

first stitch of the last round and then in the back loop of step 6. Pull the yarn through and complete the double crochet. Continue like this all the way round until all the stitches have been joined to the back loops from step 6. Remember to skip every tenth loop, as you did in step 6.

9. When the round is finished, cut the yarn and weave in the end.

10. Lastly make a tie for the waist. Work with double yarn. Using a 4.0 mm hook, make a long row of chain. When you have reached the desired length for the tie, cut the yarn and weave in the ends. A tie that goes approximately twice round your hips is about the right length to make.

11. Draw the tie in and out of every fifth treble in the top round and bring the ends together at the centre front of the skirt so they are in the right place for you to tie them when you put the skirt on.

Munk's alpaca top

I recently taught one of my best friends to crochet. I quickly figured
out which techniques and patterns to include in this book, because
while I was working on it, I always kept in mind that I should be
writing about all the things that would be useful for her to know.
I spent countless hours with her either in my little flat in Nørrebro
or outside in the summer with a cold beer, sitting with our crochet
and having deep conversations about everything and nothing.
Everyone should try it – beer, crochet and deep conversations. It
creates a very special mood, and it's very inspiring, sitting together
creating lovely crochet and sharing the journey from making the
first stitch to weaving in the ends.

I really wanted to do everything possible to ensure that she would
be well-equipped for her crochet adventure. I wanted to enable
her to crochet exactly what she was dreaming of most. The day
she came and asked me to teach her to crochet a specific sweater
turned out to be the starting signal for Munk's alpaca top. The
pattern was extremely difficult to create, but fortunately it's nice
and easy to make, so it's perfect for my beginner friend.

The top may well look a bit complicated and tricky at first glance,
but if you just take it one step at a time, I'm sure it will be fine. It is
worked in alpaca, so it's delightfully soft and warm, but at the same
time very beautiful with its big sleeves and exposed back.

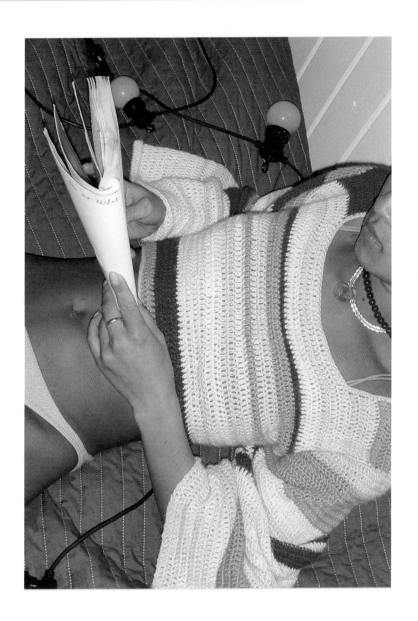

Size

Many of the measurements of the top can be adjusted as you go along. The only fixed measurement is the width of the front, which you measure at the widest part of the bust. That's the measurement on which you should base your choice of size. So take a measuring tape and measure yourself from armpit to armpit over the widest part of your bust. Be aware that the top will stretch quite a bit with use, so I recommend you go down a size or even two for this pattern.

XS: 48 cm finished chest width
S: 51 cm finished chest width
M: 54 cm finished chest width
L: 56 cm finished chest width

Materials

• 100% alpaca in DK weight
- size XS – 300 g
- size S – 350 g
- size M – 400 g
- size L – 450 g

• 3.5 mm crochet hook

Tension

10 × 10 cm = 20 trebles in width and 10 rows in height.

If you have more stitches and rows to 10 × 10 cm, change to a larger hook.

If you have fewer stitches and rows to 10 × 10 cm, change to a smaller hook.

Worth knowing before you start

Work the front of the top first. Then work the sleeves directly on the front. Lastly work a tie from each sleeve/shoulder and a tie from each corner of the bottom edge of the front. The ties create the construction of the back.

Techniques

When working back and forth in rows, each treble at the beginning of a row is replaced by 3 chain, which you use to turn the work (see pages 57–59 for more about using turning chains).

When you work in rounds for the sleeves, each treble at the beginning of a round is replaced by 3 chain. Finish each round with 1 slip stitch in the third chain you made at the beginning of the round (see page 62 if you aren't sure how to work in rounds).

The top can be worked in a single colour or with a pattern. I chose to make mine with random colour changes along the way. If you want to do the same, just change colour now and then before you start a new row. Before starting to work with colour changes, see pages 87–90 to decide which method you want to use.

Instructions
Munk's alpaca top

Front

1. Make 90 (size XS) – 96 (size S) – 102 (size M) – 108 (size L) chain plus 3 extra chain, which will function as a turning chain.

2. Work 1 treble in the fourth chain from the hook. Work trebles to the end of the row.

3. Make 3 chain, turn the work and work trebles to the end of the row.

4. Continue working trebles in rows until you have worked a total of 17 (size XS) – 18 (size S) – 20 (size M) – 21 (size L) rows. My version of the top is cropped. You can of course make it longer if you wish. If so, continue working in rows until you reach your desired length, measured from the bottom to the armhole.

5. When you have worked all the rows of trebles, cut the yarn and weave in the ends so you're ready to shape the armhole. Cast off

for the armhole in the first row. Whichever size you are making, prepare to work the armhole as follows: Skip 7 trebles at one side and start a new row of trebles in the eighth stitch of the previous row. Work trebles along the row, but don't work into the last 7 stitches of the previous row.

6. Cut the yarn and start a new row at one side by skipping 2 trebles and working 1 treble in the third stitch of the previous row. Work trebles along the row, but don't work into the last 2 stitches of the previous row. Repeat this step a total of 1 (size XS) – 2 (size S) – 3 (size M) – 4 (size L) times.

7. Cut the yarn and start a new row at one side by skipping 1 treble and working 1 treble in the second stitch of the previous row. Work trebles along the row, but don't work into the last stitch of the previous row. Repeat this step a total of 1 (size XS) – 1 (size S) – 1 (size M) – 2 (size L) times.

Make the entire front first.

Work an edging of double crochet to hide all the loose ends.

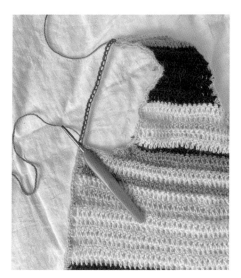

Make a row of chain from the outer corner of the shoulder down to the corner of the armhole.

Work trebles in rounds to make the sleeve.

8. You have now finished the shaping for the armhole edge. Work 6 (size XS) – 7 (size S) – 8 (size M) – 9 (size L) rows of trebles without shaping.

9. Now work the sides of the neck edge, which finishes up at the shoulder. Start at one side and work trebles over the first 18 (size XS) – 19 (size S) – 20 (size M) – 21 (size L) stitches. Turn the work and work back and forth in rows over the stitches you have just crocheted until you have worked a total of 12 (size XS) – 13 (size S) – 14 (size M) – 15 (size L) rows. Cut the yarn, weave in the ends. Turn work and repeat this step on the other side.

10. You have now made the whole of the front. Finish by working double crochet al the way round this piece to give it a neat edge. At each corner work 3 double crochet in the same corner stitch. It is important to space the double crochet evenly, so the front doesn't begin to curl up. If you have made lots of colour changes, there will be a large number of loose ends hanging from the work. Instead of weaving them all in, you can work the double crochet over them, fastening in the ends as you work the edging.

Sleeves

You begin the sleeves by making a row of chain from the shoulder edge down to the armhole. After that you work trebles in rounds.

1. Start by counting how many double crochet you worked on one armhole. Count from the bottom edge of the start of the armhole up to one shoulder. I ended up with 50 double crochet for a size XS. Take the number of double crochet you worked in the armhole and halve it. This gives you the number of chain you need to work from the shoulder down to the corner of the armhole. So for the top I made, I had to make 25 chain.

2. Join a new strand of yarn with a slip knot up in the corner of the shoulder front (see page 89 for how to join a strand with a slip knot). Make the row of chain with the number of stitches you want (see step 1 of this section for how to calculate the number of stitches) and attach it to the corner of the armhole with 1 slip stitch.

3. Make 3 chain, which count as the first treble, and work 1 treble in each chain and each double crochet so you will end up working in rounds. End the first round of the sleeve by working 1 slip stitch in the top chain at the beginning of the round. You have now worked the start of the sleeve. You make the rest of the sleeve by working rounds of 1 treble in each stitch. Remember to start each round with 3 chain and finish it with 1 slip stitch in the top chain.

4. Try the top on occasionally in order to measure the sleeve length and stop working rounds when you think the sleeve is the perfect length for you. Cut the yarn and weave in the ends.

5. Make the sleeve on the other side by repeating steps 2–4.

Ties at the back of the neck

Work the back neck ties starting from each sleeve. They are held in place on the front shoulders.

1. Start on one of the sleeves by working a row of trebles in the chain you made in step 1 of the sleeve. Start the row of trebles down by the armhole and work up towards the shoulder.

2. When you reach the shoulder, make a slip stitch where the last treble meets the shoulder.

Work slip stitches up the shoulder before you turn the work.

The tie at one side.

3. Work 3 slip stitches along the shoulder. These are instead of the 3 chain you would usually make as a turning chain.

4. Turn the work and work trebles to the end of the row, making 2 decreases at the end of the row (see page 71 if you aren't sure how to decrease in trebles).

5. Turn the work with 3 chain and work 2 decreases at the beginning of the row, before working trebles all the way up to the shoulder and repeating steps 2–4.

6. Continue in this way, working 2 decreases at the end of the row furthest from the shoulder.

7. When you can no longer fasten the row to the shoulder, continue working back and forth with normal turning chains.

8. Work back and forth in rows with 2 decreases until the tie is the width you want. The tie on the top I made ended up being 4 trebles wide.

9. When you don't want the tie to get any narrower, work back and forth in rows until it has reached the desired length – it needs to be long enough to tie together with

the other tie at the back of your neck. Cut the yarn and weave in the ends. My ties ended up being 75 cm long.

10. Make a second tie by repeating steps 1–9 at the other side.

Ties at the waist

1. Work a long row of chain at one bottom corner of the front. Stop when this chain is long enough to tie at the back in the centre to another tie of the same length (you will have to imagine this!).

2. Work the first treble in the fourth chain from the hook and work a treble in each chain all the way back to the front.

3. When you reach the front where your row of chain ends, work a slip stitch in the front, cut the yarn and weave in the ends. My tie ended up being 75 cm long.

4. Make a second tie by repeating steps 1–3 on the other side.

Bobo dress

The beautiful singer and actress Jane Birkin, who sadly passed
away in 2023, has always been a huge style icon for many people,
including me. I am deeply fascinated by her feminine French style.
I have a picture of her on my wall, where it has hung for many
years, and it's the inspiration for this dress. In this photo, Jane
Birkin is walking with her longtime partner, the French musician
Serge Gainsbourg, at her side, through the middle of what looks
like a posh party. In the background is a waiter carrying a tray
of cigars. All the guests around the couple are wearing lovely
dresses and dinner jackets. But of course, the focus of the picture
isJane Birkin and her inordinately beautiful lace dress with its
low neckline. It's the very photo that inspired me to try to make
my own version of the famous white dress. I gave my dress a little
bohemian twist with bigger sleeves, and it's also shorter. The name
Bobo is a contraction of Bourgeois-Bohemian, a name originally
given to a social group in France with bourgeois values and
bohemian lifestyles. One day I want to try to recreate a full-length
version of Birkin's gorgeous white dress.

Size

To find out which is the right size for you, measure yourself around the widest part of your hips. The instructions will explain how to achieve the length you fancy, so the lengths given are only for guidance and can always be adjusted. Your hip measurement is what is important when choosing your size.

XS – 90 cm hip – 70 cm length
S/M – 108 cm hip – 82 cm length
M/L – 126 cm hip – 93 cm length

Materials

• 100% cotton in 4 ply weight
- size XS – 500 g colour A – 50 g colour B
- size S/M – 550 g colour A – 50 g colour B
- size M/L – 600 g colour A – 50 g colour B

• 3.0 mm crochet hook

Tension

10 × 10 cm = 19 trebles in width and 11 rows in height.

If you have more stitches and rows to 10 × 10 cm, change to a larger hook.

If you have fewer stitches and rows to 10 × 10 cm, change to a smaller hook.

Worth knowing before you start

You make the back of the dress first, then the front, and then you join the two pieces together. The sleeves are worked directly from the armholes at either side of the dress. To finish, you work borders around the neck edge, the ends of the sleeves and the bottom of the dress.

Techniques

When working back and forth in rows, each treble at the beginning of a row is replaced by 3 chain, which will be used to turn the work (see pages 57–59 for more about turning chains).

When working in rounds for the sleeves, each treble at the beginning of a round is replaced by 3 chain. Finish each round with 1 slip stitch in the third chain you worked at the beginning of the round (see page 62 for more about how to work in rounds).

Instructions
Bobo dress

Back

1. Make 92 (size XS) – 110 (size S/M) – 128 (size M/L) chain plus 3 extra chain, which function as the first treble.

2. Work 1 treble in the fourth chain from the hook and 1 treble in each of the next 5 chain, so you have a total of 7 trebles. *Make 2 chain, skip 2 stitches and work 1 treble in the third stitch. Make 2 chain, skip 2 stitches and work 1 treble in each of the next 13 stitches.* Repeat from * to * to the end of the row, noting that the last repeat ends with 1 treble in each of 8 stitches, not 13.

3. Noting that you have already worked the first round of all the charts in step 2, work across chart A.1 once and then chart A.2 a total of 5 (size XS) – 6 (size S/M) – 7 (size M/L) times. Finish by working chart A.3 once. You will find the charts on page 257 (see pages 75–77 if you're not sure about working from charts). Remember to replace the first treble of each row with 3 chain.

4. When you have worked charts A.1, A.2 and A.3 a total of 13 (size XS) – 15 (size S/M) – 17 (size M/L) times, cut the yarn and weave in the ends. You can make the dress longer by continuing to work the charts until you have reached your desired length.

Front

1. Start the front in the same way as the back by repeating steps 1–3.

2. When you have worked charts A.1, A.2 and A.3 a total of 7 (size XS) – 8 (size S/M) – 9 (size M/L) times, starting from the next row you only work over the first 39 (size XS) – 39 (size S/M) – 57 (size M/L) stitches (still following charts A.1, A.2 and A.3). If you are making your dress longer than I did in the instructions, you must work the same number of extra rows on the front as you did on the back before dividing the front. Continue working the rows of the charts on the 39 (size XS) – 39 (size S/M) – 57 (size M/L) stitches of this side until you have worked charts A.1, A.2 and A.3

Create the pattern by following the chart on page 257.

Start making the deep neckline by working in rows on one side.

Work in rounds to make the sleeves.

Crochet a border around the neck in a different colour, then work borders around the bottoms of the sleeves and the dress in that colour.

a total of 6 (size XS) – 7 (size S/M) – 8 (size M/L) times. Cut the yarn and weave in the ends.

3. Now you have completed one side of the front. With the right side of the front piece facing you, count 39 (size XS) – 39 (size S/M) – 57 (size M/L) stitches in from the left side of the piece, join the yarn here, and repeat step 2, and then you will have completed the second side of the front.

Joining the front and back

1. Now join the front to the back. Place the two 2 pieces together and start by working across one shoulder from the outer edge to where the shoulder of the front stops for the neck edge. Cut the yarn and weave in the ends. Now join the second shoulder in the same way, cut the yarn and weave in the ends. If you aren't sure which method to use to join the seams, see pages 92–94 to read about the various options.

2. Now join the sides of the dress. Work up from the bottom corner, leaving the last 14 cm (size XS) – 16 cm (size S/M) – 18 cm (size M/L) open for the armhole. Cut the yarn, weave in the ends and repeat at the other side of the dress.

Sleeves

1. Now make the sleeves. Start by joining the yarn at the bottom of one armhole.

2. Work 3 chain, which count as the first treble, and work trebles all the way round the armhole. As there are no clear stitches to work into, work trebles evenly spaced around the armhole. Work a total of 72 (size XS) – 72 (size S/M) – 90 (size M/L) trebles, remembering that the 3 chain count as 1 treble. Finish the round with 1 slip stitch in the third chain you worked at the beginning of the round.

3. Now work only chart A.2 in rounds a total of 4 (size XS) – 4 (size S/M) – 5 (size M/L) times horizontally. Note that this time the row marked with a star must be worked as the first round (see page 76 for more about working in rounds from charts, if needed).

4. When you have worked chart A.2 a total of 9 (size XS) – 9 (size S/M) – 9 (size M/L) times vertically, or depending on how long or short you want your sleeves, cut the yarn and weave in the ends.

5. Work the second sleeve by repeating steps 1–4 at the other side of the dress.

Borders and ties

To finish, you work the borders and the little ties on the front. You can make the borders in the same colour as the dress or in a contrasting colour, as seen in the dress here.

1. Join the yarn at the bottom of the dress. *Make 1 chain and then 1 double crochet in the same stitch. Work 1 double crochet in each stitch all the way around the bottom of the dress. Finish the round with 1 slip stitch in the first chain you worked.* Repeat from * to * 1 more time. Cut the yarn and weave in the ends.

2. Work the borders at the bottom of the sleeves in the same way as step 1.

3. Work the border around the neck edge in the same way as step 1. However, there are no clear stitches to work into here, so work double crochet evenly spaced. It is best not to make too many double crochet, as that may cause the edge of the work to curl.

4. Finish by making the 2 little ties in the middle of the low neckline. Start by putting on the dress. At one side of the neckline, just under your bust, insert a double strand of yarn using a slip knot (see page 89 for how to join a new strand of yarn with a slip knot). Make a row of chain and when it measures about 20 cm, or whatever length you want your tie to be, cut the yarn and tie a knot in the end. Repeat this step at the other side.

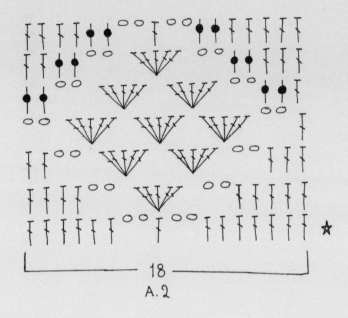

18

A.2

★ = Work this round

O = Chain

⊤ = Treble in the stitch

● = Treble in the chain arch

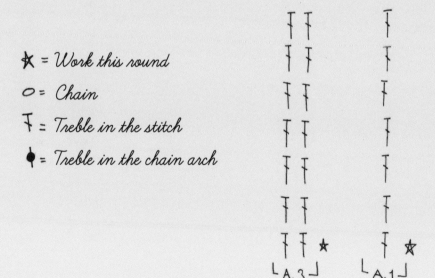

A.3   A.1

Inspiration

The ten films listed here have particularly impressed me and they have also influenced my crochet designs. These films don't necessarily feature any specific crocheted items, but they all have a special vibe that I wanted to recreate.

1. *Goodfellas* (1990)

A great gangster film, the action of which takes place from the 1950s to the 1980s. This film is responsible for many of the colour combinations I put together for the crochet items in this book. The costumes are absolutely crazy and the colours are to die for!

2. *True Romance* (1993)

This was the first film my uncle and I watched in our beloved film club. A sweet, different kind of love story that has a special place in my heart. The scenes are so beautiful, with a great vibe that I immediately wanted to recreate in my crochet.

3. *The Big Lebowski* (1998)

A lovely, funny film that is basically about a man who only wants to get his ruined favourite rug replaced. It is set in the 1990s, but the majority of the action takes place in a gorgeous bowling alley that is clearly inspired by the 1950s. The music, production design and indeed the entire film are absolutely inspiring – this movie makes me want to put on a great crochet outfit before I go out and order myself a White Russian.

4. *The Talented Mr. Ripley* (1999)

An incredibly beautiful film set in the 1950s on Italy's Amalfi Coast. Because of its summery, southern European atmosphere, this film was my inspiration for the beach skirt on page 224, among other things.

5. *Blow* (2001)

I think this is actually my favourite film. It's just crazy and everybody should see it! In brief, this film is about the American cocaine market in the 1970s. Also, a small part of the film takes place in Mexico, and I love Mexico. The costumes are so delightful, and many of the crochet items in which I use yellow and blue together were inspired by this film. I don't exactly know why, but those are the colours that come to me when I watch it.

6. *No Country for Old Men* (2007)

You wouldn't immediately think that this film would provide crochet inspiration, but it did for me, and maybe it will inspire you too. It's about a drug deal that goes wrong and a man who now has all the money being hunted by an insane murderer. The images in the film are very striking, as a large part of the action takes place in the empty deserts of Texas.

7. *The Imaginarium of Doctor Parnassus* (2009)

This is one of the first films I saw that really made an impression on me. With this film, it was definitely the whole vibe and the dreamy nature of the plot that inspired me. There is an old-fashioned circus atmosphere that I drew inspiration from in both my crochet and my interiors. The dream world of the film and the special universe of the theatre and circus are all filled with delightful impressions.

8. *Call Me by Your Name* (2017)

I'm sure many people associate this film with summer, Italy and a delightful 1980s atmosphere. I won't tell you what the film is about, because you really have to watch it, if you haven't seen it already. Every time I've crocheted bikinis I've had this film in mind. Be careful about watching it in winter, because it will leave you yearning for summer.

9. *Bohemian Rhapsody* (2018)

One of the first times I crocheted anything, I put on *Bohemian Rhapsody*. I had to keep putting down my crochet in order to pause the film so that I could take photos of the characters' costumes and homes. If you look closely, you can see some lovely crochet items in the background on several occasions. The film is about the band Queen and their lead singer, Freddie Mercury, who was a huge style icon for many people, including me.

10. *Once Upon a Time in Hollywood* (2019)

This film takes place in 1969 in Los Angeles – so we already have a fantastic setting. It also features a group of hippie girls, who often appear wearing little crochet tops or carrying crochet bags. Pay particular attention to the scene where these girls are crossing the road after having been out partying. One of them, a character called Pussycat, is wearing a lovely white top under her overalls. However, the most iconic crochet top in the film is the rainbow halterneck that she wears most of the time that she is on screen. This very same top was the inspiration for the pattern on page 214.

Index

Originally published by Gyldendal NonFiktion, Klareboderne 1-3, 1001 København K, Denmark

First published in Great Britain in 2024 by Ilex Press, an imprint of Octopus Publishing Group Ltd Carmelite House 50 Victoria Embankment London EC4Y 0DZ www.octopusbooks.co.uk

An Hachette UK Company www.hachette.co.uk

The right of Rose Svane to be identified as the author of this Work has been asserted in accordance with the Copyright, Designs & Patents Act 1988.

ISBN 978 1 78157 898 8

A CIP catalogue record for this book is available from the British Library.

Printed and bound in China

10 9 8 7 6 5 4 3 2

Cover, illustrations and layout: Pia Storm
Illustrations pages 40-95: Sofie Kampmark
Photo page 14: Armin Tehrani
All other photos and illustrations: Rose Svane

For Ilex Press
Commissioning Editor: Ellie Corbett
Senior Editor: Alex Stetter
Copy Editors: Lisa Pendreigh, Rosee Woodland
Translation from Danish by Rae Walter in association with First Edition Translations Ltd, Cambridge, UK
Art Director: Ben Gardiner
Layouts adapted by Jeremy Tilston
Assistant Production Manager: Allison Gonsalves